Write for College:
An Overview

What is *Write for College*?

Write for College is a handbook for writing, thinking, and learning. It is not a textbook, not a "rhetoric," and not just a reader. It's a resource for writers who, regardless of their writing tasks, want a source they can get into quickly for the information they need. That way the writer's work remains central, not the book. Below are other qualities that distinguish *Write for College* from other handbooks.

- Writing is linked to critical thinking, researching, reading, listening, and speaking in order to help students acquire the skills they need to become independent, lifelong learners.

- The handbook's content, reflecting both contemporary theory and instructors' time-tested wisdom, stresses academic excellence.

- The handbook doesn't just tell, it shows— providing models of sentences, paragraphs, essays, and research papers.

- Information on writing, speaking, learning, and studying helps students learn in all their classes.

- Guidelines and models for a wide range of writing tasks—along with extras like math and chemistry tables, the U.S. Constitution, and world maps—help instructors in all disciplines to use writing to teach.

Who is *Write for College* designed for?

While the handbook is aimed at college-level writing performance and college-level culture, it's suitable for your students if you are one of the following:

- Freshman composition instructor or teacher at a college or university

- High-school Senior English or Advanced Placement instructor

- Teacher or professor in any college or advanced high-school class in which writing is a vital part of the instruction

- Tutor or supervisor in a school or college writing center

How can *Write for College* be used?

Primary Text ● *Write for College* can be used as the primary resource for writing and language learning. Instructors can use it as a teaching text to initiate writing and learning. Students can use it as a reference book when they are working on any writing and learning projects.

All-School Handbook ● *Write for College* also works well as an all-school handbook. Because it is portable, user-friendly, and comprehensive, students will find it an invaluable resource not only in their English and writing classes, but across the curriculum as well. It will help students become better students in all their course work.

What are the key sections of *Write for College*?

Write for College is divided into seven major sections, each dealing with a key area of writing and language learning:

The Writing Process emphasizes techniques that help writers move through the steps of generating and selecting material, to the steps of drafting and revising, and finally to the steps of polishing, editing, and proofreading.

The Basic Elements of Writing deals with specific challenges in the writing process—things like refining one's style, identifying and avoiding common ailments in style, writing and expanding sentences, developing strong paragraphs, and learning the basics of the college essay. Various types of business writing are also covered.

The Forms of Writing offers help for composing 23 forms (personal, report, analytical, and persuasive) of writing commonly assigned in college. There's also a section on writing about literature. Each form is introduced by a one-page set of guidelines followed by both a student model and a professional model.

The Research Center clearly and thoroughly describes the steps in the research process. Sample parenthetical references and bibliographic entries are given for MLA and APA research styles. Information is included on using and citing electronic sources.

The Tools of Learning includes information about improving reading and note-taking skills, critical listening, and test-taking skills. Special emphasis is also given to formal speaking and to building logical arguments.

The Proofreader's Guide is a handbook within a handbook, answering any questions a writer might have concerning punctuation, grammar, usage, and mechanics.

The Almanac includes full-color maps, the U.S. Constitution, helpful metric conversion charts, and the periodic table of the elements, as well as other useful lists to make *Write for College* an across-the-curriculum reference.

How does *Write for College* teach writing?

The *Write for College* handbook presents brief guidelines that lead writers through the writing process, "Quick Guides" that offer helpful tips, and numerous models of how students and professionals write.

For writers trying to solve simple, immediate problems, *Write for College* presents short sections of information easily accessed with the index. For writers trying to solve more complex, extensive problems, *Write for College* presents entire chapters and in-depth information on the writing process from prewriting and drafting to editing and publishing.

How should you use the *Write for College Instructor's Manual*?

In addition to the chapter overviews and objectives, the extensive instructor's notes for the 23 forms of writing provide the basis for planning a writing syllabus. The writing workshops can be used as suggested in the instructor's notes, in writing groups, or independently as needed. The cross-curricular writing assignments provide starting points for making writing a vital part of learning in any discipline. Use the MUG Shot sentences and paragraphs to give students structured practice in editing and proofreading.

How is *Write for College* organized?

Information in the handbook is organized so that it's accessible—students find what they need without having to sift through whole sections or chapters. This quick tour highlights major points of interest in the handbook.

- ◉ Creative, Contemporary Design
- ◉ Stimulating Illustrations
- ◉ Student and Professional Models
- ◉ User-Friendly Text
- ◉ Numerous Guidelines, Checklists, and Charts
- ◉ Comprehensive Proofreader's Guide
- ◉ Cross-Curricular References
- ◉ Easy-to-Use Index

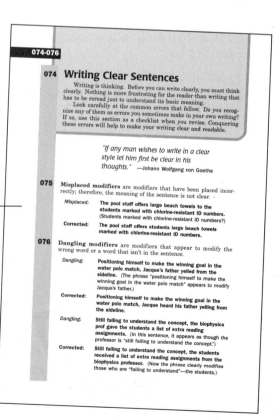

187

Analytical Writing

It's 10 p.m., and you finally force yourself to look at the assignment sheet for Sociology 101. *Analyze one aspect of computer technology in terms of its effect on modern society*, it says. You flash back to those happy times in high school when you cranked out creative essays on the life of a shoelace and what you would do if you won the lottery. Now, you're not sure you can analyze your lunch, much less anything to do with computers.

Actually, there's nothing mysterious about analytical writing. It's simply a type of writing that requires some high-octane thinking. In analysis, you interpret information rather than report on it; you form new understandings rather than simply give the facts. You might, for example, evaluate the impact of computers on education. Or you might examine a problem related to computers in the workplace.

WHAT'S AHEAD

Analytical writing covers a lot of territory, as you will see in this section. Included are guidelines and models for essays that explain, compare, classify, define, evaluate, and so on. Remember to approach your analytical writing with the proper mind-set, with a genuine interest in your subject, and with the patience to explore it carefully and thoroughly.

> *"Writing is how we think our way into a subject and make it our own."* —William Zinsser in *Writing to Learn*

Chapter Introductions

Engaging introductory copy gains the students' attention and previews the guidelines and examples that follow.

074-076

074 **Writing Clear Sentences**

Writing is thinking. Before you can write clearly, you must think clearly. Nothing is more frustrating for the reader than writing that has to be reread just to understand its basic meaning.

Look carefully at the common errors that follow. Do you recognize any of them as errors you sometimes make in your own writing? If so, use this section as a checklist when you revise. Conquering these errors will help to make your writing clear and readable.

> *"If any man wishes to write in a clear style let him first be clear in his thoughts."* —Johann Wolfgang von Goethe

075 **Misplaced modifiers** are modifiers that have been placed incorrectly; therefore, the meaning of the sentence is not clear.

Misplaced: **The pool staff offers large beach towels to the students marked with chlorine-resistant ID numbers.** (Students marked with chlorine-resistant ID numbers?)

Corrected: **The pool staff offers students large beach towels marked with chlorine-resistant ID numbers.**

076 **Dangling modifiers** are modifiers that appear to modify the wrong word or a word that isn't in the sentence.

Dangling: **Positioning himself to make the winning goal in the water polo match, Jacque's father yelled from the sideline.** (The phrase "positioning himself to make the winning goal in the water polo match" appears to modify Jacque's father.)

Corrected: **Positioning himself to make the winning goal in the water polo match, Jacque heard his father yelling from the sideline.**

Dangling: **Still failing to understand the concept, the biophysics prof gave the students a list of extra reading assignments.** (In this sentence, it appears as though the professor is "still failing to understand the concept.")

Corrected: **Still failing to understand the concept, the students received a list of extra reading assignments from the biophysics professor.** (Now the phrase clearly modifies those who are "failing to understand"—the students.)

Topic Numbers

Topic numbers (rather than page numbers) make it easy for students to find specific information.

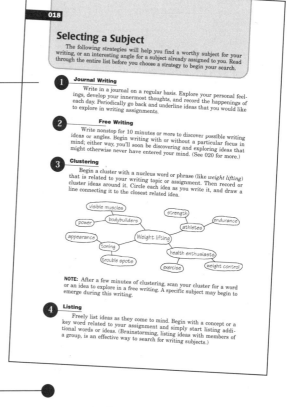

Guidelines and Checklists

Concise guidelines and checklists provide students with effective pointers as they develop their writing and learning.

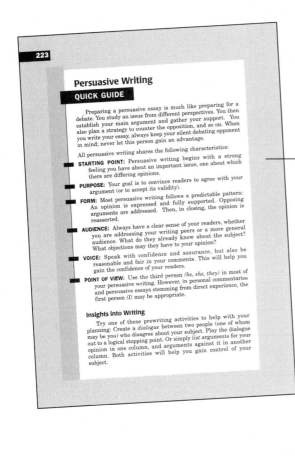

Quick Guides

Many chapters contain a "Quick Guide," establishing a handy frame of reference for the information that follows.

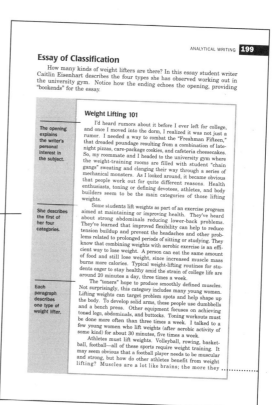

Student and Professional Models

A student or professional model complements each set of writing guidelines. The models are annotated to help students understand how the writing is put together.

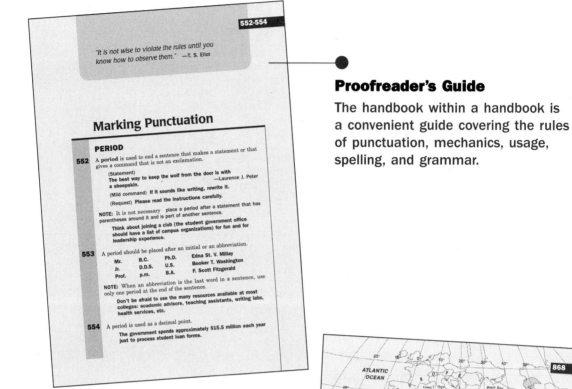

552-554

> *"It is not wise to violate the rules until you know how to observe them."* —T. S. Eliot

Marking Punctuation

PERIOD

552 A **period** is used to end a sentence that makes a statement or that gives a command that is not an exclamation.

(Statement)
The best way to keep the wolf from the door is with a sheepskin. —Laurence J. Peter

(Mild command) **If it sounds like writing, rewrite it.**

(Request) **Please read the instructions carefully.**

NOTE: It is not necessary place a period after a statement that has parentheses around it and is part of another sentence.

Think about joining a club (the student government office should have a list of campus organizations) for fun and for leadership experience.

553 A period should be placed after an initial or an abbreviation.

Mr.	B.C.	Ph.D.	Edna St. V. Millay
Jr.	D.D.S.	U.S.	Booker T. Washington
Prof.	p.m.	B.A.	F. Scott Fitzgerald

NOTE: When an abbreviation is the last word in a sentence, use only one period at the end of the sentence.

Don't be afraid to use the many resources available at most colleges: academic advisors, teaching assistants, writing labs, health services, etc.

554 A period is used as a decimal point.

The government spends approximately $15.5 million each year just to process student loan forms.

Proofreader's Guide

The handbook within a handbook is a convenient guide covering the rules of punctuation, mechanics, usage, spelling, and grammar.

868

AFRICA

Important Extras

Maps, charts, and conversion tables are included in the almanac to enhance the cross-curricular use of the handbook.

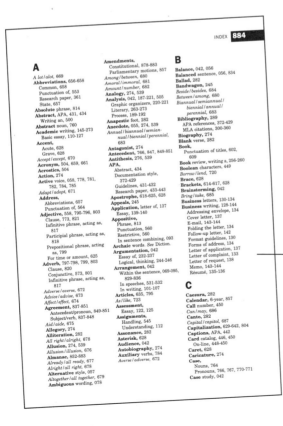

INDEX 884

Indexed Information

Every important concept covered in the handbook is listed by topic number in the index. (There are no page numbers in *Write for College.*)

Section-by-Section Overview

The Writing Process

Rationale: Our purpose in this section is to impress upon students that writing is a highly individual process of exploring and shaping meaning, rather than an end product. Each section offers a number of strategies for tackling each phase of the writing process: prewriting, drafting, revising, editing, and proofreading. The chapters describe steps in the process and encourage students to work and rework their writing until it is strong and clear.

Chapter Summaries

One Writer's Process (003-016)

Objectives:

- To give students a basic guide for the writing process.
- To show students how the writing process can work.

"One Writer's Process" shows the steps student Mark Klompien worked through in the development of an assignment for his composition class. Have students note the wording of the assignment and ask them to determine the "key" phrases ("personal experience" and "a current cultural, social, or political issue") that would help generate some ideas for the assignment. Also, to help students work from the general to the specific, you could point out that considering a possible "cultural, social, or political issue" first might lead to

remembering a "personal experience," which in turn could supply the focus for the assignment. Emphasize the usefulness of clustering, the collecting strategy represented under "Collecting Ideas" (004). Point out the Quick Guide (016) that students can use as a review of the process whenever they face a writing project.

Explain to students that writing is a recursive process that may involve many more changes than are illustrated in Mark's work.

A Guide to Prewriting (017-024)

Objectives:

- To help students understand the prewriting process.
- To give students strategies for selecting and shaping writing ideas.

Author Joyce Carol Oates refers to connecting with "your true subject" as the key to effective writing. Most writers would agree; the problem is making that connection. This chapter features a series of strategies that students may refer to whenever they need prewriting help. Make sure that students understand two important aspects of the prewriting process: (1) how to select a subject, and (2) how to focus their efforts.

Journal writing, free writing, clustering, etc., are all ways of "priming the pump," or getting ideas to flow. Sometimes a degree of patience is needed: it can take time for the tugs of daily responsibilities and obligations to dissipate before the more creative thinking process "kicks in." Encourage students to be patient, to keep writing; eventually, the ideas will come and the focus will follow.

Workshop Connection: "Discovering Interesting Subjects," p. 76

A Guide to Drafting (025-028)

Objectives:

- To help students understand the drafting process.
- To provide students with strategies for developing drafts.

The strategies in this chapter help students with different aspects of the drafting process: writing openings, advancing the thesis, and writing endings. There is no one "perfect" way to write drafts. This chapter suggests options that have worked for many writers. Students should try various ideas until they find what works best for them.

Workshop Connection: "Finding a Voice," pp.82-83

A Guide to Revising (029-036)

Objectives:

- To help students understand the revising process.
- To provide students with revising strategies.

It is essential that students understand that effective writing is nearly always the product of thorough revising. This chapter covers all aspects of the revising process from using basic revising guidelines to peer reviewing. "Revising on the Run" (030) comes from Peter Elbow's recommendation for those who have very little time to make changes in their writing. "Peer Reviewing" (034), designed to encourage student writers to review each other's work, offers valuable guidelines for maintaining productive working relationships.

Workshop Connections: "Advising in Peer Groups," p. 96; "Evaluating Style," p. 97; "Evaluating Writing," p. 98

A Guide to Editing and Proofreading (037-040)

Objectives:

- To help students understand the functions of editing and proofreading.
- To provide students with strategies for fine-tuning their writing and checking it for accuracy.

This chapter provides checklists that students can use during editing and proofreading. It ends with a list of common writing errors. Help students understand the difference between editing and proofreading: (1) editing is improving the revised writing; (2) proofreading is correcting the finished product.

Workshop Connections: "Proofreading: Usage," p. 123; "Proofreading: Review," p. 124

NOTE: At the beginning of the course, you may give a simple diagnostic test/survey of students' knowledge of basic mechanics, usage, and grammar. Using this information plus students' awareness of their own particular writing weaknesses, you can refer students to various MUG Shot sentences and paragraphs for self-remediation, or you can incorporate occasional discussion and review of these basic skills into the class work.

Writer's Resource (041-045)

Objectives:

- To provide a useful glossary of writing terms.
- To acquaint students with some of the more commonly used foreign words and phrases in college-level reading.

This chapter presents two compact lists of extremely useful words and phrases. Familiarity with the writing terms will provide a common vocabulary for both you and your students. The list of foreign words and phrases will help students in their understanding of more sophisticated college-level reading.

The Basic Elements of Writing

Rationale: We developed the "Basic Elements of Writing" to help students establish a solid foundation for all their writing. The information in "Writing with Style" and "Making Sentences Work" will help students express themselves clearly and correctly. The guidelines and examples in "Developing Strong Paragraphs" and "Mastering the College Essay" will help students learn how to carry their fundamental skills to a higher level. "Taking Care of Business" is a unique section designed to assist students in the everyday responsibilities of their lives, from writing business letters to composing memos and sending e-mail.

Chapter Summaries

Writing with Style (046-067)

Objectives:

- To help students develop their own unique and personal styles of writing.
- To assist students in learning how to avoid biased writing.

This chapter addresses style from many points of view including the traits of effective style, common ailments of style, and techniques for improving style. Discuss the importance of style and note how students can use the lists and examples in this chapter to refine their writing. "A Fair Writing Style" shows students what to include (and what to avoid) in order to achieve fairness in their writing.

Making Sentences Work (068-095)

Objectives:

- To focus students' attention on the sentence as a key element in their writing.
- To assist students in writing clear, effective sentences using a variety of techniques.

This chapter provides many examples of common sentence problems, together with clear explanations of how to avoid them. The end of the chapter discusses more sophisticated sentence writing with examples of expanded and cumulative sentences. Discuss how students can use material in this chapter when revising their own writing or when responding to the writing of others.

Developing Strong Paragraphs (096-109)

Objectives:

- To demonstrate the importance of the paragraph as a major organizational writing unit.
- To show the importance of using support for ideas, and how to organize and develop that support.

One of the major problems in student writing is the lack of support for the ideas presented. This chapter features several options for developing supporting details. Patterns for presenting details are modeled in various types of paragraphs. The last page of this chapter presents a "Quick Guide" for easy reference.

Mastering the College Essay (110-127)

Objectives:

- To provide a guide for writing effective college essays.
- To help students identify qualities of good essay writing.

Following the previous chapter on paragraph development, this section shows students how to organize their ideas, how to get started, and how to fine-tune what they've written. Emphasize that understanding the assignment (112) is the pivotal starting point for an effective college essay, and review how Mark Klompien (in "One Writer's Process," 003-016) identifies key phrases in the assignment to guide his writing.

Taking Care of Business (128-144)

Objectives:

- To help students appreciate the purpose and importance of business writing.
- To present guidelines and models for writing that is part of the job-search process.

Beginning with a "Quick Guide" for handy reference, this chapter uses models and specific guidelines to help students carry out the day-to-day responsibilities of college life.

The Forms of Writing

Rationale: Our purpose in this section is to provide students with guidelines and models for writing 23 forms of essays commonly assigned in college. The forms are arranged into the following five categories: personal writing, report writing, analytical writing, persuasive writing, and writing about literature. Guidelines for each form lead students through the process of (1) searching and selecting a topic, (2) generating the text, (3) writing and revising the essay, and (4) evaluating the final draft. The guidelines are followed by model essays—the first usually written by a student, and the second written by a professional writer.

NOTE: This manual (pages 43-70) includes detailed lesson plans for teaching each of the forms of writing mentioned above. Every lesson plan includes a description of the writing form, strategies for introducing the form, techniques for guiding students through the writing process, and references to writing workshops (in this manual) for refining skills used in the process.

The Research Center

Rationale: One of the primary goals of higher education is to develop critical thinking skills. Research writing, while valuable in itself, is one of the best ways to develop these skills. Learning to narrow a topic, organize information, and present the finished product in a clear and interesting manner will prepare students for many different tasks and responsibilities in their lives.

Chapter Summaries

Writing the Research Paper (284-293)

Objectives:

- To update students with the latest developments in research writing.

- To guide students through the steps in the research process.

This chapter takes the student step-by-step through the process of writing a research paper. Instructors need to support students through the inevitable trial-and-error experience, reminding them that thinking and writing are not done "in straight lines," but often in circles or back and forth. These guidelines offer clear and reassuring help for the most uncertain writers.

 There's a helpful, in-depth discussion of writing a thesis statement that students can review whenever they begin a writing project.

Writing Responsibly (294-299)

Objectives:

- To show students the need for careful, mature thinking.

- To provide clear, useful examples of how to avoid plagiarism.

One of the most important skills students learn through research writing is decision making. It is not enough to merely find information. Students must also make decisions about which information to use and how to use it. This is a difficult but ultimately rewarding part of the process, because it lifts students' thinking to new levels of maturity. You may want students to practice the techniques for avoiding plagiarism by having them all write (and then share) summaries of the same paragraph.

MLA Documentation Style (300-361)

Objectives:

- To familiarize students with the MLA (Modern Language Association) style of documentation.

- To provide examples of MLA documentation, including a section on electronic sources.

The examples of MLA documentation provided in this chapter were the best available when the handbook was printed. The section on "Computer Network Sources" (355-360) deals with a still-evolving aspect of the research process.

 Students may go to the Web site "thewritesource.com" for additional MLA examples and updates for MLA electronic-source citing.

MLA Research Paper (362-371)

Objective:

- To familiarize students with the MLA style of documentation in a student research paper.

A great deal can be learned by (1) reading the paper in its entirety to grasp its purpose and then (2) rereading, observing the marginal notes. The topic is current, the sources are up-to-date, and the author presents a balanced perspective.

APA Documentation Style (372-429)

Objectives:

- To familiarize students with the APA (American Psychological Association) style of documentation.
- To provide examples of APA documentation, including a section on electronic sources.

As with the MLA documentation, *Write for College* presents examples of APA documentation.

 Students may go to the Web site "thewritesource.com" for additional APA examples and updates for APA electronic-source citing.

APA Research Paper (430-443)

Objective:

- To familiarize students with the APA style of documentation in a student research paper.

The APA style differs from the MLA in some key aspects. Therefore, the "Questions and Answers" (431-432) are especially helpful. *Note:* You should inform students that individual professors may differ on their research-style requirements. Flexibility and adaptability are the watchwords, so advise students to use common sense.

Searching for Information (444-455)

Objectives:

- To assist students in learning how to use a well-equipped college library.
- To help students evaluate information and detect bias.

Students become frustrated when they can't find the information that they need. Most college libraries have well-trained reference staff to assist student researchers; however, you may have to encourage students to seek assistance. You should be familiar with the library's holdings, policies, services, and technology.

Using Electronic Sources (456-461)

Objectives:

- To provide information on current technological services.
- To assist students in using electronic sources.

"Tips for Traveling on the Information Super-highway" offers a commonsense approach to doing information searches. You may want to point out that "Netiquette" offers advice for dealing appropriately with Internet sources.

Writing with a Computer (462-467)

Objectives:

- To provide a review of the writing process as done on a computer.
- To explain computer and Internet terminology.

The list of computer and Internet terms is valuable. The review of the writing process with its "Upside/Downside" approach balances some students' view that using computers is always an advantage.

Using the Writing Center (468-472)

Objective:

- To show students how a writing center works and how they can use it effectively.

Tutors in campus writing centers help students see their papers more objectively. "Tips for Getting the Most Out of the Writing Center" and job descriptions for the advisor/tutor and the student are useful. Finally, a brief discussion of on-line writing labs (OWL's) points students to ways of getting help through computer connections.

The Tools of Learning

Rationale: Although college is a higher-level learning experience, basic learning skills need to be polished, refined, and retooled on an ongoing basis. This section of *Write for College* takes students to the next level of those skills, to help them achieve success in college and later in life.

Chapter Summaries

Reading to Learn (473-480)

Objectives:

- To provide students with strategies and guidelines for reading to learn.
- To provide memory strategies to help students remember what they read.

The introduction to this chapter comes from a real-life discussion with students about how to read a classic assignment. For many, "active reading" (as described here) and "passive reading" are unknown distinctions; all reading is considered the same because it seems the same. A few comments relevant to this introduction will help your students understand that learning is a job that requires the proper preparation and tools. They also will appreciate an honest admission that even we English instructors don't effortlessly commune with Chaucer, Milton, or Angelou; we, too, must use these same skills.

 INSIDE info The insights into "Reading a Poem" provide a good starting point for students who are writing explications.

Critical Listening and Note Taking (481-492)

Objectives:

- To provide effective strategies for listening and note taking, involving both left- and right-brain functions.
- To present some tips and cautions about electronic note taking.

The information in this chapter is presented in a clear, straightforward style. These strategies are effective because they've been used for years and they work. An especially useful feature is the "mind map," which gives students who are more right- than left-brained ideas for note taking. The underlying philosophy for all these strategies is this: To listen, you need to be an alert, active learner.

Writing to Learn (493-500)

Objectives:

- To offer students the techniques that will help them learn.
- To illustrate four important writing-to-learn activities.

Some people say, "I don't know what I think until I write it." This may sound silly, but it makes a good deal of sense. Writing things down forces us to think about them, if only to make the writing coherent. Writing is, above all, a thinking activity, and it promotes higher-level thinking skills. Learning logs, summaries, paraphrases, and abstracts are activities that aid students in making sense out of what they read and hear. This is analytical writing at its most effective.

Taking Tests (501-512)

Objectives:

- To help students improve their performance on essay, objective, and standardized tests.
- To indicate the benefits of study groups and how to form them.

For those who believe that they're simply "bad test takers," this chapter can be great therapy. Reviewing for tests and forming a study group can be great strategies for success. Some students prefer solitary study, while others thrive on group discussions. Key terms used in essay tests are presented, along with a clear example of how to organize the essay answer. Finally, a list of tips for coping with test anxiety is presented.

 INSIDE info Pointers for taking objective tests will help students avoid careless errors.

Building a College-Sized Vocabulary (513-528)

Objective:

- To provide clues, tips, and strategies to help students build a better vocabulary quickly.

This handy reference begins with a "Quick Guide" that lists strategies for vocabulary building. The remainder of the chapter expands on these strategies, concluding with a fairly extensive list of prefixes, suffixes, and root words that will give any student a better command of English.

Speaking Effectively (529-542)

Objectives:

- To provide guidelines to help students prepare and deliver a speech or report.
- To define terms distinguishing style and techniques used in public speaking.
- To provide guidelines for preparing for and doing an interview.

Studies have shown that public speaking is one of our most-feared activities. This chapter includes guidelines for writing, rehearsing, and delivering three kinds of speeches: impromptu, outline, and manuscript. It also contains a model manuscript speech. You may introduce the chapter by reading the first three pages and stressing that the steps in "Preparing to Give a Speech" (530) are important for all three forms of speeches. Use the guidelines and the model to help students understand how to develop and present a speech. The last section, "Conducting Interviews" (541-542), is especially useful for college students who will do interviews to find information for research assignments, and to pursue job opportunities.

Succeeding in College (543-551)

Objectives:

- To introduce students to basic issues dealing with campus life.
- To provide a glossary of terms common to the college experience.

Academic life is only one part of a college student's learning experience. For most students, discovering newfound freedom in living away from home, lacking an externally structured schedule, and making new friends and decisions have the potential for risk, excitement, and reward.

Proofreader's Guide

Rationale: The "Proofreader's Guide" is placed near the end of the handbook in order to emphasize the fact that writing and language learning should not begin with the study of grammar. The beginning of good writing is thinking and ideas, not the mechanics of syntax and punctuation. Although mechanics are important, they should be kept in perspective.

Chapter Summaries

Proofreader's Guide (552-851)

The "Proofreader's Guide" is divided into five parts: "Marking Punctuation," "Checking Mechanics," "Using the Right Word," "Understanding Our Language," and "Using the Language." "Understanding Our Language" deals with the parts of speech; "Using the Language" thoroughly covers sentence construction and variety, as well as the importance of agreement. Each one of the five parts contains explanations and examples to illustrate the basic rules.

Almanac

Rationale: The "Almanac" helps make *Write for College* an all-purpose reference book that students can use across the curriculum, and that teachers can use to integrate the curriculum.

Chapter Summaries

Almanac (852-883)

This section includes useful tables and lists (including metric conversion tables for weights and measures), a 6-year calendar, common parliamentary procedures, the periodic table of the elements, full-color maps of the world, and the full text of the U.S. Constitution.

Writing and Learning Across the Curriculum

Setting Up a Cross-Curricular Writing Program

> *"The productive use of language, and especially writing, is a valuable tool for learning for all students in all subjects at all ages."*
>
> —John S. Mayher, Nancy Lester, and Gordon M. Pradl

Understanding the Purpose

Journal writing, dialogues, and stories—these particular forms of writing have traditionally been associated exclusively with the English curriculum. But not any longer. There are more and more instructors in all content areas who have their students explore their thoughts and feelings in journals, confront challenging ideas in dialogues, and develop content-related fictional pieces.

These instructors realize that writing plays a central role in the learning process. Writing by its very nature gets students actively and thoughtfully involved in their work whether they are studying conflict resolution, photosynthesis, or local government. It helps them understand and remember important concepts. It makes them more appreciative of course content and curious to learn more. And it gives students control over their own learning.

The Ultimate Learning Tool

Writing is such an important learning tool that all instructors must make room for it in their curriculum. The critical question no longer is why students should be writing, but rather how much writing they should be doing and in what forms. That's why we developed this section.

We can think of no better way for instructors to pool their efforts than to promote writing and learning. It is a no-lose situation. The more proficient students become as writers, the more able they are to learn. We agree with Nancie Atwell's statement in *Coming to Know* (Heinemann, 1990): "In the best of all possible worlds, language study should be part and parcel of the entire school curriculum. The whole school day should be a learning workshop."

Identifying the Basic Types of Writing

There are many reasons for asking students to write; the four reasons that follow deserve attention in any schoolwide writing program:

Writing to Learn

As was mentioned earlier, writing to better understand or learn new concepts is one of the most beneficial reasons to have students write. It is also the easiest type of writing to implement. (Refer to "Writing to Learn" in the handbook and pages 17-22 in this manual for a list of easy-to-implement writing-to-learn activities.)

Journal Writing

Writing to explore personal thoughts and feelings in a journal works as well in social work or science as it does in English composition or literature. Students who engage in journal writing become much more in tune with their course work and much more comfortable with the act of composing. (See "A Closer Look at Journal Writing" on pages 23-24 in this section for more information.)

Writing to Share

Writing to share learning also plays an important part in a schoolwide writing program. Students approach writing with more interest, care, and concern if they know that they have an interested audience with whom to share their ideas and research. In the process of sharing their ideas, students naturally learn from one another. Any kind of writing can be shared: lab reports, essays, project reports, position papers, or free writings.

Writing to Show Learning

Writing to show learning is the traditional reason instructors have had their students write. When students compose summary paragraphs, write literary analyses, draft reports, or answer essay-test questions, they are writing to show learning. While writing to show learning was once the primary reason to have students write, it is now only one of many reasons to initiate writing.

A Closer Look at Writing to Learn

"Writing to learn focuses on better thinking and learning. To be sure, students who use writing as a way of learning often produce better written products, but this is a side benefit, not the chief purpose."

—Anne Ruggles Gere

Q. What exactly is "writing to learn"?

A. Writing to learn is a method of learning that helps students get more out of their course material. It is thinking on paper—thinking to discover connections, describe processes, express new understandings, raise questions, and find answers. It is a method that students can use in all courses—and even in the workplace.

Q. What is the purpose of writing to learn?

A. The main purpose is better thinking and learning. (Better writing is a by-product.) This is why writing to learn is not limited to English instructors.

Q. What makes writing to learn work?

A. Writing is uniquely suited to encourage abstract thinking. The linearity of writing—one word after another—leads to more coherent and sustained thought than simply thinking or speaking. Also, writing allows all students to respond, including those who are reluctant to answer out loud.

Q. What are the advantages of writing to learn for students?

A. Writing to learn provides students with a way of learning, not just a set of facts. It forces students to personalize—to internalize—learning so that they understand better and remember longer. It also encourages higher-level thinking skills such as analysis, synthesis, and evaluation.

Q. What are the advantages for instructors?

A. Instructors using writing to learn will (1) see learning, thinking, and writing improve among their students; (2) notice improved communication, rapport, and motivation as students become more independent and more actively involved in the learning process; and (3) come to rely less and less on "writing to show learning," which needs to be graded.

Q. How do you go about beginning a writing-to-learn program?

A. First of all, there is no one "program" for writing to learn. Instructors can begin with the writing-to-learn activities (493-500) in the *Write for College* handbook. After working with this section, both students and instructors should have a good idea of what writing to learn is all about.

Then instructors must select from the wide variety of activities available those that best suit their needs and the needs of their students. Once an activity is selected, students need to understand they are "writing to learn," not "writing to show learning." If they understand that they are not writing simply to please their instructor, but to personalize and better understand information, you are on your way.

Q. What kinds of topics are good for writing to learn?

A. Any topic that is worth knowing or thinking about is a good writing-to-learn topic. Instructors in subject areas where writing does not usually occur need only identify the "language components" in their subjects and select a writing activity that will work within the context and setting of the course.

Q. What kind of writing is considered writing to learn?

A. Journals, learning logs, lists, observations, summaries, paragraphs, surveys, and any other writing activity that helps students personalize and make meaning out of what they are attempting to learn are all writing-to-learn activities.

Q. What does an instructor have to know before using writing to learn in the classroom?

A. Very little. The information in this guide will give you more than enough information and ideas to get started. Remember, too, that there is no "right way" to use writing to learn; it is up to the instructor to select those activities that are best suited to meet students' needs and accomplish course goals.

Q. Are there any highly recommended activities that can be used immediately?

A. Yes, learning logs, stop 'n' write, and admit slips (or exit slips) are excellent activities to start with.

Q. What other materials would be helpful in setting up a writing-to-learn program?

A. You can refer to any of the resources listed below (which were used in compiling the information in this manual). Unless otherwise noted, the titles are Heinemann/Boynton-Cook publications.

> ### Recommended Reading:
>
> *A Community of Writers*
> — Steven Zemelman and
>   Harvey Daniels
>
> *Learning to Write/Writing to Learn*
> — John S. Mayher, Nancy Lester,
>   Gordon M. Pradl
>
> *Roots in the Sawdust: Writing to Learn across the Disciplines*
> — Anne Ruggles Gere, ed.
>   (Available through NCTE)

Writing to Learn: 10 Things You Should Know

Write for College contains a special section on "Writing to Learn." Students are given the background necessary to begin using writing to learn, especially in learning logs and summaries. The following information provides both instructor and student with additional writing-to-learn ideas.

1. Writing to learn may be the best way we know to achieve the overall goal of education: providing students with an effective way of thinking and learning for a lifetime.

2. Writing to learn is a method of learning that helps students get more out of their material. It enables instructors and students to focus on the process of learning—thinking—rather than on the product of learning—factual information. (In the process, factual information is learned.)

3. Writing to learn is student centered. The ideas and motivation for writing come mainly from the students, who are quick to realize that writing can lead to more effective learning (and better grades).

4. Writing to learn enables students to personalize/internalize learning so that they can better understand and remember.

5. Writing to learn encourages abstract, higher-level thinking. The linearity of writing—one word after the other—leads to more coherent and sustained thought than mere thinking or speaking.

6. Writing-to-learn activities differ from traditional writing activities in several important ways:

Writing to Learn	Formal Writing
• spontaneous	• planned
• short	• lengthy
• exploratory	• authoritative
• expressive	• transactional
• informal	• formal
• personal	• impersonal
• unedited/unfinished	• polished
• ungraded	• graded

7. Writing to learn allows all instructors to be instructors of writing and thinking. Writing is both an internal (content) and external (mechanics) activity. Since all instructors are experts in their content area, they are well equipped to help students with the internal side of writing. They can help students gather, organize, and react to the content of their writing. (By using their handbooks, students are able to do much of their own editing and proofreading.)

8. Learning works best as a dialogue, not a monologue. Writing to learn makes it possible for an instructor to carry on a dialogue with 25 students at once.

9. There is no "right way" to use writing to learn. Students should be introduced to a variety of activities for which they can use writing to learn both in and out of the classroom. They should be allowed to experiment and to create writing-to-learn activities of their own. In fact, the only requirement is that the risk of grading must be eliminated; only then will uninhibited thinking and personalizing take place. The list on the following pages contains activities that can be used effectively in a variety of situations.

10. Writing to learn is not the same as writing to show learning. Its purpose is learning, not showing what has already been learned. Writing to learn should be thought of as a tool for learning, a tool that works best when it is comfortable in the hands of the user. Students should use the language they "think in"—language that is as close to their everyday speech as possible. Compare the two samples below in which the instructor had asked each student to write a short response to a reading about diffusion. The paragraphs were to show, in the students' own words, their reactions to the material as well as what they had learned. Otto wrote this:

> Substances leave and enter cells by diffusion and osmosis. Diffusion is when molecules move from an area of greater concentration to an area of lesser concentration. Concentration is the amount of material per unit of volume. The more molecules, the greater concentration. For sugar and protein to enter cells, they must break apart into substances that can dissolve in body fluids. Molecules move through the cell membrane by diffusion. Osmosis is the diffusion of liquid through a membrane. Food and oxygen diffuse from the blood through the cell membrane into the cell. Cell wastes diffuse back through the cell membrane into the bloodstream.

Virtually all of the language here is that of the text; it offers none of Otto's personal reactions nor makes any connections with his life. Otto will most likely forget what he has written within a relatively short time. In contrast, Emily wrote this:

> In reading this section I thought of the lab that I did on diffusion. I knew something about diffusion, but I didn't really know it. I thought of how neat it was that these molecules seemed to have a brain that tells them where to go. It's like they knew and have always known what to do. How to diffuse

Emily does not summarize or repeat the material but interprets and reacts to it by connecting it to previous experiences and giving her personal response. In doing so she opens up a new range of possible questions; for instance, what is the "brain" behind the process of diffusion? Emily has started making the material part of her own thinking, the goal of writing to learn.

Writing-to-Learn Framework

The framework below lists different writing-to-learn activities according to the basic type of thinking involved in each one. For example, when a student is keeping class minutes, he or she is basically recording information. When a student is developing an observation report, he or she is describing a process or an object. This framework should help you decide which writing-to-learn activities to assign for different purposes in your classroom. (Most of the activities listed here are described on the following pages.)

PERSONAL WRITING	
Recording	Learning Logs Class Minutes Active Note Taking
Gathering	Brainstorming First Thoughts Listing
Remembering	Focused Writings
SUBJECT WRITING	
Describing	Observation Report
Reporting	5 W's and H
Corresponding	Admit/Exit Slips Correspondence
Informing	Student Teachers How-to Writing
Searching and Researching	Key Word Summing Up
ACADEMIC WRITING	
Synthesizing	Bio-Poem
Clarifying	Metacognition Instant Versions
Evaluating	Question of the Day Stop 'n' Write
PERSUASIVE WRITING	
Focusing	Clustering/Completions
Reviewing	Writing Groups
Arguing and Proving	Unsent Letters Facts/Values List

WRITING-TO-LEARN ACTIVITIES

The following activities can be used to promote writing to learn. Instructors (and students) should experiment with a variety of activities and then decide on several that would best suit a particular course.

Active note taking: Students are asked to divide a page in half. On the left side, they record notes from their reading, and on the right side, they write comments or questions about the material they have read. This written dialogue makes note taking much more meaningful and provides students with material for class discussion. Here are some types of comments students may use:

- a comment on what memory or feeling a particular idea brings to mind

- a reaction to a particular point that they strongly agree or disagree with

- a question about a confusing concept

- a paraphrase of a difficult or complex idea

- a discussion of the importance or significance of the material

- a response to an idea that confirms or questions a particular belief

Admit slips: Admit slips are brief pieces of writing (usually on half sheets of paper) that can be collected as "admission" to class The instructor can read several aloud (without naming the writers) to help students focus on the day's lesson. Admit slips can be a summary of an assigned reading, questions about class material, requests for instructors to review a particular point, or anything else students may have on their minds.

Bio-poems: Bio-poems help students synthesize learning because they must select precise language to fit into this form. *(Note:* Even though the bio-poem is set up to describe "characters," it can also be used to describe complex terms or concepts such as *photosynthesis, inflation,* etc.) Bio-poems encourage metaphorical and other higher-level thinking. An adaptation of a bio-poem could follow this pattern:

BIO-POEM

Line **1.** First name, term, or concept
Line **2.** Four traits that describe the character, term, or concept
Line **3.** Related to ....
Line **4.** Lover of ....(list three things or people)
Line **5.** Who (or which) feels .... (three items)
Line **6.** Who (or which) needs ....(three items)
Line **7.** Who (or which) fears..........................(three items)
Line **8.** Who (or which) gives ....(three items)
Line **9.** Who (or which) would like to see ....(three items)
Line **10.** Resident of ....
Line **11.** Last name or a synonym for the term or concept

Brainstorming: Brainstorming (list storming) is writing done for the purpose of collecting as many ideas as possible on a particular topic. Students will come away with a variety of approaches that might be used to further develop a writing or discussion topic. In brainstorming, everything is written down, even if it seems at the time to be a weak or somewhat irrelevant idea.

Class minutes: One student is selected each period to keep minutes of the class (including questions and comments) to be written up for the following period. That student can either read or distribute copies of the minutes at the start of the next class. Reading and correcting these minutes can serve as an excellent review, as well as a good listening exercise.

Clustering: Clustering is a special form of writing to learn that begins by placing a key word (nucleus word) in the center of the page. For example, suppose students were to answer an essay question asking for an explanation of the phrase, "eighteenth-century rationalism." *Rationalism* would be the obvious nucleus word. Students would then record words that come to mind when they think of rationalism. They should record every word, circle it, and draw a line connecting it to the closest related word.

Completions: By completing an open-ended sentence (which the instructor or other students provide) in as many ways as possible, students are pushed to look at a subject, problem, or situation in many different ways. Writing completions also helps students focus their thinking on a particular idea.

Correspondence: One of the most valuable benefits of writing to learn is that it provides many opportunities for students to communicate with their instructors. Instructors should set up a channel (e-mail, memo exchange, etc.) that encourages students to communicate freely.

Dialogues: Students create an imaginary dialogue between themselves and a character (a public or historical figure, for example) or between two characters. The dialogue will bring to life much of the information being studied about the life or times of the subject.

Dramatic scenarios: Writers are projected into a unit of study and asked to develop a scenario (plot) that can be played out in writing. If the unit is on decision making, for example, students might put themselves in President Truman's shoes the day before he decided to drop the atomic bomb on Hiroshima. The scenario would include whatever discussions they think this dramatic decision may have entailed.

Exit slips: Students are asked to write a short piece at the end of class in which they summarize, evaluate, or question something about the day's topic. Students turn in their exit slips as they leave the classroom. Instructors can use the exit slips as a way of assessing the success of the lesson and deciding what needs to be reviewed before going on to the next topic.

Facts/values lists: When a new topic is being introduced, students write down everything they "know" to be a fact on the left side of their papers, and everything they "believe, feel, or suspect" about the topic on the right. Not only will students become immediately involved with the new topic, but sharing these lists is also bound to provide some interesting introductory material for the whole class.

First thoughts: Students write or list their immediate impressions (or what they already know) about a topic they are preparing to study. These writings will help students focus on the task at hand and will also serve as a point of reference to measure subsequent learning.

Focused writings: Writers are asked to concentrate on a single topic (or one particular aspect of a topic) and write nonstop for a certain amount of time. Like brainstorming, focused writing allows students to see how much (or how little) they have to say on a particular topic.

Free writing: Students write nonstop on a particular subject for a certain amount of time. During a free writing, students often discover things about a subject they weren't aware they knew. They often discover connections or personal associations that were not at first obvious. (See "Selecting a Subject" in your handbook.) Directed writing is a variation on free writing that explores six modes of thinking: describing, comparing, associating, analyzing, applying, and arguing for or against. (See "Shaping a Subject" in your handbook.)

How-to writing: Students are asked to write instructions or directions on how to perform a specific task. This will help students both clarify and remember. Ideally, students would then be able to test their writing on someone who does not already know how the task is performed.

Journals: Journals are places for students to keep their personal writings, including any of the writing-to-learn activities in this list. Often called "learning logs," journals allow students to record their impressions, questions, comments, discoveries, etc., about any subject. (See "Writing in Learning Logs" in *Write for College*.)

Key word: Students can be asked to write about a key word or concept connected to the class. By doing a focused writing in which they attempt to "define" a key word or "summarize" a concept, students have an opportunity to bring together and internalize the information that is being presented.

Learning logs: A learning log is a journal (notebook) in which students keep their notes, thoughts, and personal reactions to the subject. (See "Learning Logs" in *Write for College* for guidelines for keeping a learning log and sample learning-log entries.)

Listing: Freely listing ideas as they come to mind is another effective writing-to-learn activity. Students can begin with any idea related to the subject and simply list all the thoughts and details that come to mind. Listing can be very useful as a quick review or progress check.

Metacognition: Students are asked to write about their own thinking process, including where in the process they understood (or got lost) for the first time and how they went on from there. "Thinking about thinking" is especially useful in math, science, and business.

Observation reports: The classic observation report has long been a staple in science labs. This report can be equally useful in other disciplines. The objective is to collect data from close observation of objects, processes, and events. However, it is important to remember that, as with any writing-to-learn activity, an observation report should be written in language that allows students to personalize or internalize the information.

Predicting: Students are stopped at a key point during a class period and asked to write what they think will happen next. This works especially well with topics that exhibit strong cause and effect relationships.

Question of the day: Writers are asked to respond to a question (often a "What if . . . ?" or "Why?") that either is important to a clear understanding of the topic or prompts students to think beyond the obvious.

Stop 'n' write: At any point during a class discussion, students can be asked to stop and write. This will allow students a chance to evaluate their understanding of the topic, to reflect on what has been said, and to question anything that may be bothering them. These writings also help instructors assess how the lesson is progressing. (See "Predicting.")

Student teachers: One way to encourage students to personalize or internalize class material is to have them construct their own word problems, scenarios, and discussion questions (which can be used for reviewing or testing). This is a great way to replace routine end-of-the-term questions with questions that students actually wonder about or feel are worth answering.

Summing up: Students are asked to sum up what was covered during a particular class by writing about its importance, a possible result, a next step, or a general impression.

Unsent letters: Letters can be written to any person on any topic related to the subject being studied. Unsent letters allow students to become personally involved with the subject matter and enable them to write about what they know (or don't know) to someone else, imagined or real.

Warm-ups: Students can be asked to write for the first 5 or 10 minutes of class. The writing can be a question of the day, a free writing, a focused writing, or any other writing-to-learn activity that is appropriate.

Writing groups: Students can benefit greatly from working in groups. The writing that comes from a group discussion or brainstorming session can be either an individual or a collaborative effort. Group response to the writing can help students further clarify their thinking and writing. Group writing works especially well for quick summaries or short observation reports. (See "Peer Reviewing" in *Write for College* for guidelines and strategies for group critiquing sessions.)

A Closer Look at Journal Writing

Instructors in various disciplines focus attention on covering concepts and on helping students master skills in a specific course. And rightfully so. However, what often gets lost in this content shuffle is the opportunity for students to reflect upon or internalize what they have just learned.

Connecting Thoughts and Feelings

To our way of thinking, students benefit greatly from a personal engagement in learning. They should have every opportunity (and should be encouraged) to explore their thoughts and feelings about all of their course work.

> *". . . thoughts and feelings do not operate as independent domains, but rather wrap themselves around each other in helical fashion."*
> —Dan Kirby and Carol Kuykendall,
> *Mind Matters*

Journals in Every Classroom

Because journal writing binds content (facts, figures, concepts, theories, formulas) together with student feelings (reactions, wonderings, questions), it plays a significant role in making learning happen. Students can immerse themselves intellectually and emotionally in their learning, whether they are studying equations in algebra or deforestation in science, prejudice in sociology or poetry in literature class. It provides a way for students to work things out for themselves, to take an active role in their learning. In short, it is a powerful learning tool that deserves a place in every classroom.

Implementing Journal Writing

Journal writing can be easily implemented. Students need only a notebook and encouragement. The handbook offers students guidelines to get them started. (See "Writing in Learning Logs.") Students should write in their journals on a regular basis—perhaps two or three times a week, 10 minutes at a crack. Finally, give students the freedom to write about anything on their minds that is somehow related to their course work. That's it.

Writing Prompts for Journals

Instructors who work with journals often provide students with one or two prompts each time they are expected to write. Students can use one of the prompts as a starting point for their writing, or they can write about a topic of their own choosing. Sample prompts for major content areas are listed below and on the following page. (Use this as a guide for compiling your own list of prompts.)

History, Sociology, or Politics

- **How has the shift to a global economy affected your life?**

  In a free-writing activity, discuss the ways your life and your future career are affected by a "world without borders."

- **It has been said, "The best form of government is a benevolent monarchy."**

  Define the phrase "benevolent monarchy" and then explain what you find to be the strengths and weaknesses of the concept.

- **Which is more critical in the development of human beings, heredity or environment?**

  Defend your position in this controversy.

- **Discuss nuclear family units (parents and children only) and then compare them with larger tribal communities.**

  What factors have contributed to small family units?

- **"What's good for General Motors is good for the country."**

  Explain what this quotation means and then agree or disagree with it, giving your reasons.

- **In 1941 President Franklin D. Roosevelt mentioned four freedoms worth fighting for: freedom of speech and expression, freedom of worship, freedom from want, and freedom from fear.**

  Are any of these ideals worth fighting for and possibly dying for today? Think about some of the major conflicts/wars going on in the world. Discuss your answers in small groups.

Mathematics

● **Make a list of problems mathematicians have not been able to solve.**

Pick two and tell why each is hard to solve.

● **Mathematics exists throughout nature.**

Identify three mathematical concepts that apply to animals, the earth, the environment, weather, microscopic life, or space. Then describe how you have studied these concepts.

● **Write a story problem involving positive and negative numbers.**

Get into a group with three classmates and invite them to solve your story problem. (P.S. Make sure *you* can solve it.)

● **Mathematics has a long history.**

From the Great Pyramid builders of Egypt to the Druid priests who constructed England's Stonehenge, people throughout history have used mathematics. Choose one five-year span in history when mathematics helped the advancement of civilization. Write a journal entry highlighting the use of mathematics during that time.

● **Imagine that you are an astronomer watching a meteor fly through space.**

List three mathematical questions for which you need answers in order to understand what you are watching. Explain why each of the three is important.

Science

● **Explain to a six-year-old the difference between a solid, a liquid, and a gas.**

● **Write a historical fiction journal entry that a famous inventor could have written.**

Be sure that your writing covers an invention from its inspiration to the final discovery.

● **Name science-related problems in industry.**

Imagine that you head an industrial business facing one such problem. Write a letter to your board of directors describing the strengths and weaknesses of two possible solutions.

● **If there is in fact a crisis in science education today, how *should* schools teach science?**

Free-write ideas that might actually be used in your class this year.

● **What is the scientific method?**

In your own words, explain each step in the scientific method. Then explain how this method is used to find cures for various diseases.

Communication

● **In any kind of writing it's important to know your audience.**

Write journal entries about your day for two audiences: a friend and your grandmother.

● **Name some fallacies of thinking that you should avoid in your thinking and writing?**

Write of ads you have seen recently in magazines or on TV and explain how one or more fallacy was used to sell the product.

● **If communication is critical, what should schools be teaching young people in this area?**

Write about what you wish you knew how to do better and what you think will be required of you in the workplace.

● **Keep a journal for a week, noting and commenting on both the positive and negative communication that you encounter.**

Engineering

● **"Nobody can avoid technology; it affects every aspect of life. Those unable to use it face a lifetime of menial work."**

Agree or disagree and give your reasons.

● **What are some social consequences of the computer revolution?**

Discuss ways computers change the job world.

● **What does the future hold?**

Write a daily journal entry for a person your age, living in the year 2295.

● **Before phones, videos, and TV, people relied on written communication. Now, thanks to e-mail, faxes, laptops, and the Internet, people are writing again.**

Discuss this new role of the written word.

● **"Virtual-reality experience, as it becomes more accessible, could significantly erode the participant's reading skill."**

Agree or disagree and give your reasons.

Writing Assignments

Instructors in most disciplines often assign very formal types of writing—primarily paragraphs, reports, and essays. There's nothing wrong with this standard fare, but there are so many other ways for students to share what they have learned. They can write advertisements, news stories, feature articles, editorials, letters, manuals, scripts, and so on.

Me, a Writing Teacher?

Instructors don't have to be accomplished fiction writers, journalists, or technical writers to bring these new forms into their classrooms. The role of instructors in any discipline should be to help students develop their ideas. The instructors are the experts in their respective fields, and they can put this expertise to good use by guiding students as they select, investigate, and work with writing ideas. By helping students with the ideas in their writing, instructors are serving their students as well as themselves. When it comes to shaping and refining their writing, students will find helpful writing, revising, and proofreading guidelines in their handbooks.

Our Recommendations

Why do we recommend that instructors vary the types of writing they assign? If all we ever ate for lunch were egg salad sandwiches, we would soon lose our taste for them. The same holds true for writing. You can't expect students to have much of an appetite for writing if their diet never varies.

But there is another reason. Assigning paragraphs and reports generally promotes what James Britton calls "classificatory writing—or writing which reflects information in the form teachers and textbooks present it." Put in another way, the paragraphs and reports students write often reflect only what they have been told or what they have read, not what they have personally thought about and learned.

What's needed are opportunities for students to write in more creative and critical ways. Generally speaking, writing letters, editorials, plays, and stories is a much more thoughtful enterprise than writing basic paragraphs and reports. These alternative forms demand more commitment on the part of students and get them more intellectually and emotionally involved in their writing. They help students understand and apply information rather than simply restate it.

As mentioned earlier, students also need every opportunity to write for real audiences other than their instructors. Writing letters (to send), editorials (to submit), brochures (to send to actual audiences), and plays (to perform) provides such opportunities. When students know that there is a real audience out there, they are more apt to put forth their best efforts. Their writing is a reflection of their very own thinking. It only makes sense that they would want it to reflect a positive image.

Writing Activities

Write for College provides specific writing ideas for instructors in all content areas. Immediately following this page are writing assignment worksheets that instructors can use as a resource when planning writing activities. We suggest instructors establish guidelines for their own writing activities in much the same way. In addition, later in this section, instructors will find a list of more than 60 ideas for writing assignments across the curriculum. These writing ideas cover several content areas, from science and history to English and mathematics.

Ready-Made Activities

And certainly not to be forgotten are all of the other ready-made activities promoting writing and learning in *Write for College*. There are enough activities to be shared among all the content areas. Perhaps the history department could focus on journal writing (discussed in this section), the biology department and math department on introducing writing-to-learn techniques (discussed on pages 17-22 of this guide), and the English department on the different forms of communicating and writing in *Write for College*.

DESIGNING WRITING ASSIGNMENTS

The following discussion will help instructors design assignments that promote writing as a meaning-making process.

Writing Assignment:

In a paragraph, identify three ways in which consumers can produce less waste.

DISCUSSION: It's a sure bet that students' responses to such an assignment will be very predictable . . . and, unfortunately, very dull. ("There are three main ways to cut down on consumer waste . . .") The assignment follows the age-old formula: question and answer, tell and retell, stimulus and response. It requires little genuine thinking on the part of students, and, therefore, they gain very little from the experience. A meaningful and memorable learning experience it is not. Compare this assignment with the one that follows.

Writing Assignment:

Convince a friend, parent, or neighbor—real or imagined—that he or she should produce less waste.

Subject: The problem of consumer waste
Purpose: To convince someone to change his or her behavior
Form: Friendly letter, editorial letter, memo
Audience: The person you want to convince plus your reading audience (your writing group or classmates)
Voice: Speak with confidence
Point of View: Third person

Evaluation:

◉ Does the writing sound convincing? (Are main points supported by specific details?)

◉ Does the writing form a meaningful whole, moving smoothly and clearly from one point to the next?

◉ Will readers appreciate the treatment of this subject?

DISCUSSION: So many more possibilities are presented to students in the second example. They can't follow a formula or simply repeat what they have already been told or what they have already read. Instead, they have to apply their knowledge about the subject matter in a specific context that they help to design. They have to decide whom they are going to address, what they are going to say, and how they are going to say it. It is the type of assignment that can lead to real learning.

Getting Started

In *Learning to Write / Writing to Learn* (Heinemann-Boynton/Cook, 1983), authors John Mayher, Nancy Lester, and Gordon Pradl provide a basic three-step process to help instructors develop well-conceived writing assignments.

1. First, instructors should define or identify learning objectives in their disciplines that could be facilitated by writing. The authors stress that these must be genuine objectives (to help students relate the problem of consumer waste to their immediate world, for instance) rather than activities.

2. They should then design writing assignments to help students achieve the objectives.

3. Lastly, instructors should establish guidelines or criteria to evaluate the outcome of the students' work. (Evaluation should focus on writing as a process of exploring and shaping.)

Special Note: A planning sheet for designing well-conceived writing assignments is on the next page.

What to Consider

When designing a writing task, consider that a meaningful writing assignment . . .

● places students at the center of the writing and learning process,

● evolves from either general instruction or prewriting activities,

● is clearly described to the students,

● directly or indirectly addresses the elements of effective communication (subject, audience, purpose, form, research), and

● offers options for the students.

ASSIGNMENT PLANNING SHEET

SUBJECT:

PURPOSE:

FORM:

AUDIENCE:

VOICE:

POINT OF VIEW:

PREWRITING ACTIVITIES: (Prewriting activities are especially important if the writing assignment does not stem from information or concepts already covered in the class.)

1.

2.

GUIDELINES FOR EVALUATION: (Focus on inventiveness and depth of thought more than on correctness.)

1.

2.

HELPING STUDENTS WITH . . .

Classroom Writing

How can instructors create the proper climate for writing in their classrooms? In *Investigate Nonfiction* (Heinemann, 1989), Donald Graves gives the following advice:

- Allow students to work on their writing in class. Students need sustained periods of time to work. (That is why many instructors conduct writing workshops in their classrooms.)

- Reserve class time for sharing sessions. When students talk about their writing in progress, they often put more effort into their work. (It also helps if they get to write about subjects that genuinely interest them.)

- Encourage (or require) students to keep track of their writing progress in journal or log entries. (This helps them maintain interest in their writing.)

- Share writing models so students can see how professionals write about business, chemistry, social work, and so on. (Discuss these models to ensure that students fully appreciate the writing.)

- Provide support throughout the writing process. For example, encourage peer feedback on first drafts. (Writing is hard work, and students need to know that someone is there to help them whenever they are struggling.)

Report Writing

When classroom reports or research papers are assigned, make sure students turn to the handbook for guidelines and a model. Also note the following suggestions made by Graves:

- Urge students to consider what they already know about a subject and what they need to find out. (This gives students a starting point for their research.)

- Advise students to use clusters (semantic webs, maps) to sort out their thoughts and feelings about their subject and to help plan and organize their writing.

- Help students test their note-taking abilities by having them discuss their notes without referring to the source text(s).

- Guide students during the recurring steps in the process of report writing. (These steps include gathering data, discussing, abstracting, and writing.)

Special Note: Instructors can't expect students to come into their classrooms completely knowledgeable and comfortable with the report-writing process. For example, if students are expected to conduct interviews, they will need guidance and practice beforehand.

- Suggest that students work a subject through at least two sequences of data gathering, discussing, and exploratory writing before they establish a definite focus for their report. (Students need to think of report writing as a process of discovery.)

- Initiate more than one report assignment throughout the school year. Some reports can be shorter than others, and not all of them have to be taken to finished form. (Proficiency comes through practice.)

Helpful Hint: For an alternative to the traditional classroom report, we suggest that students develop a personalized research paper (report) stemming from a pressing question they want answered. (Refer to "Research paper, Personal" in the handbook index for guidelines.)

Essay Writing

College students can develop thoughtful essays if instructors provide the necessary foundation for this challenging form of writing. Graves suggests that instructors prepare students in the following ways:

- Look for opportunities to have students tell stories or recount processes. (The ability to recount is strongly connected with the ability to plan and write nonfiction prose.)

- Provide many information-gathering experiences for students. (Interviewing and other firsthand data-gathering experiences like direct observation should be given priority.)

- Ask students to interpret the data they have gathered. (The foundation of effective essay writing is in its clarity and logical use of data.)

Across-the-Curriculum Writing Assignments

The writing assignments are arranged according to these disciplines: agriculture, art, biology, chemistry, environmental science, history, mathematics, political science, psychology, social work, and sociology. However, because each assignment encourages students to think about a topic in a cross-disciplinary manner, most assignments are appropriate in two or three disciplines. (All assignments can be adapted for other disciplines.)

Agriculture

Mechanics of Agriculture

Write an essay about a mechanized piece of agricultural equipment (tomato picker, potato harvester, grain combine, submerged irrigation pump, grape picker, etc.). Inform your reader about how the machine was first developed, how its design has changed over the years, and how it functions.

Ethics of Biofuels

Write a position paper in which you argue that agricultural land and crops should (or should not) be used to produce biofuels (like ethanol).

Field to Store

Go to the fresh produce department of a local grocery store, select a food item, and read the label, advertisement, or packaging to determine where the item was produced. Then write a report describing the route the item traveled from its production site to the grocery store. Include the distance traveled, time involved, number of people involved, and approximate handling and transportation cost. (You may need to question the produce manager, the store's warehouse manager, and various produce brokers to find your answers.)

Farming Then and Now

Write an essay in which you compare and contrast ancient Egyptian farming and irrigation methods with farming and irrigation methods used today.

Cost of Change

Write a paper on one farming sector (dairy, poultry, grain, fruit, etc.) explaining changes in the last 20 years in the size of operations, technology used, number of farms, number of employees per farm, and management practices. Also explain how these changes have affected nearby communities.

Contract System

Write an essay analyzing how the contract system (corporations contracting with independent farmers to produce commodities) has affected a sector of agriculture: swine, honey, grain.

Co-ops Then and Now

Write an essay on why the cooperative (co-op) movement in agriculture began. Describe the co-ops' goals and practices in the early days of the movement, and explain how and why those goals and practices may be different today.

Art

Me and My House

The newly rich Americans of the nineteenth-century often flaunted their wealth by building elaborate homes in eighteenth-century European styles. Select a fashionable house style from the 1800s, research it, and write the script for a guide who will give a tour of the home, explaining its architecture.

Have a Chair

Select a chair style to illustrate furniture design from a particular period. Then, as the builder of this chair, write an essay describing how the chair's design and construction affect its practical use, durability, and comfort. Also discuss how the chair "fits" the historical period it represents. If possible, find pictures of this chair and include them with your essay.

Meet the Artist

Choose an artist and a representative piece from a particular period. Using the artist's "voice," describe your life and your art, explaining what inspired the specific work and what affected its style. Be prepared to present your essay in class along with slides or pictures of the art.

The Difference Is . . .

Working with a classmate, choose two artists with very different styles. Then write a dramatic script in which the two people meet and comment on each other's work. Be ready to read your script in class while showing slides or pictures of both artists' work.

Step This Way, Please . . .

Prepare a brochure for visitors to one of the following: a Gothic cathedral, an Egyptian ruin, the Parthenon, the Globe Theatre, St. Peter's Basilica. Explain what is unique about this particular building as well as what is typical about it in light of the construction of its period.

Dear Mom

Write a letter to a family member in which you introduce her or him to an artist. Describe the artist and his or her work and explain why you do (or do not) like the artist's work. Support your opinion with details that will help your reader understand your viewpoint.

Photography and Painting

Look carefully at the landscape paintings of the 1850s, the photographs made with the earliest cameras, and the expressionist and impressionist paintings of the late 1800s. Then write an essay in which you explain how the invention of photography may have influenced expressionist and impressionist styles.

Biology

Technology and Ethics

Write an essay in which you (1) describe practices of a current technology; (2) explain what principles presently guide its use; and (3) identify ethical questions associated with its use. Possible subjects: subtherapeutic antibiotic therapy; animal-, plant-, and insect-growth regulators; artificial insemination; embryo transfer; embryo splitting; and cloning.

Clear Labeling

Choose three processed foods (like hot dogs or ice-cream bars). Read and study the labels, listing ingredients and other nutrition facts. Then read a few articles calling for clearly written, meaningful labels. Finally, write a paper in which you report on how the labels you studied match up to the articles' demands.

Observing and Writing

Visit an integrated wild landscape and respond to it in three types of writing: (1) journal notes in which you record your initial sense of the place, (2) formal field notes in which you record the findings of your more thorough observations, and (3) a report (to be read in class) in which you give both your personal (subjective) response and your clinical (objective) response.

Photosynthesis

Study the process of photosynthesis. In your journal, write two descriptions of the process: (1) for third-grade students who asked, "Where does oxygen come from?" and (2) for Biology 102 students who are studying the technical details for an exam.

Chemistry

Learning by Instructing

Write a set of instructions for a laboratory procedure used in your chemistry class. Then briefly note why it is essential to follow the instructions carefully in order to achieve the required outcome.

Two Sources; Two Stories

Read two versions of a newsbreaking scientific discovery that illustrates an application of chemistry: (1) a popular-press version in a magazine like *Newsweek* or *Time*, and (2) a scientific-literature version in a journal like *Nature* or *Science*. Then write a report comparing the stories in terms of content, approach, emphasis, organization, and editorializing.

Acid in Your Eye

Anyone working in a lab setting must wear protective eyewear when working with concentrated sulfuric acid. Find information on this acid, and then describe the chemical process that would result if a drop of concentrated sulfuric acid came in contact with someone's cornea.

Pushing the Author

Read an article in *Scientific American* with a critical eye. Then write a journal entry in which you pose a question for the author. It may take the following, or some other, form. "You said or suggest _____ in your article, but how do you account for _____?" In class, be ready to explain why your question is important.

Environmental Science

Saving Our Soil

Write an informative essay in which you (1) define soil conservation, (2) explain one of the following conservation methods (windbreaks, terracing, no-till agriculture, or the tolerable soil-loss approach), and (3) use the revised universal soil loss equation (RUSLE) or the wind erosion equation to explain why the method works.

Nitrogen Use and Overuse—on the Farm

Write an essay explaining what "nitrogen runoff" means, what causes it, and what implications it has for farmers who use nitrogen fertilizer to raise corn. Support your position by citing current research.

Nitrogen Use and Overuse—in Town

Write an essay explaining what "nitrogen runoff" means, and what causes it. Briefly describe the problem of nitrogen runoff on farmland, but focus your essay on nitrogen runoff in urban settings. For example, did you know that the recommended use of the leading granular lawn fertilizer adds five times more nitrogen to the soil per square foot than the average application of fertilizer on corn land?

Wind-Driven Schools

An Iowa school system is building wind turbines to provide electricity for its schools. The school superintendent argues that the project is valuable not only because the school saves money on energy, but also because teachers can use information from the turbines to teach math and science. List as many examples as you can of what these math and science lessons might be—particularly in relation to environmental science.

Danger of Extinction

Choose a creature on the list of endangered species and write a report identifying what is causing the creature's demise and what solutions could help resolve the problem.

Two Versions of One Story

Read two articles on an environmental issue—one in the popular press and one in a scientific journal. Then write an essay comparing and contrasting the two articles in terms of (1) how the problem is defined, (2) what solutions are offered, and (3) how arguments are supported with research.

Politics and the Environment

Research an environmental problem debated by politicians and write an essay identifying how political self-interest may or may not be shaping the public's understanding of what the problem is and how it can be solved.

Defend and Protect

Visit a nearby park, forest preserve, or wilderness area. Write a report based on what you observe. Then use what you have written as the basis for a brochure urging people to protect the particular area.

History

Knight Life

Write an essay comparing and contrasting the lifestyle of knights from the 800s to the 1100s with the lifestyle of knights from the 1100s to the 1300s. Give reasons for the similarities and differences.

Different Choices

Write a report comparing and contrasting the organization of a town or county in New England in the 1600s with the organization of a town or county in the Midwest in the 1870s. Give reasons for the similarities and differences.

Myth and Image

Write an essay describing the origin of a myth or an image and the way it was interpreted or used at a particular point in time. Examples: Hollywood image of Native Americans during the 1950s; European idea of Muslims during the Middle Ages; white American view of Africans and African Americans during the 1700s.

You Are Caesar

Imagine you are Julius Caesar preparing to cross the Rubicon to march on Rome. Write a letter to the Roman Senate justifying your action. Explain what rules and long-standing practice you would be breaking, why you would break them, and what the result of your march might be.

Right Around the Corner

Research the history of a building, company, church, store, or restaurant and present the findings in a news story or feature article. Present your topic from an interesting angle—start with a surprise or fascinating quotation, write as if you were the building's original architect or builder, etc.

Boom and Bust

The decades of the 1920s and 1930s provide a study in contrast. Write the condensed history of a small business operating during these two decades. If possible, base your writing on an actual business in your community.

What If . . .

Write an essay in which you work through the significance of a historical event by imagining a different outcome. Examples: (1) What if American "patriots" had lost the Revolutionary War—how might the North American continent have developed? (2) What if American research on the atomic bomb had not produced a weapon until 1947—how might the war and postwar politics have been different?

Mathematics

Learning by Summarizing

Write a one-paragraph summary of a basic concept, theory, procedure, or application. Examples: limit, integral, average value; Intermediate Value Theorem; Fundamental Theorem of Calculus; Chain Rule, Taylor Series representation; rectilinear motion; area between two curves.

Introducing Your Assignment

After doing the assigned reading in your text, write a one-page introduction to the material explaining what the topic is, why it is important, how it fits into the field, and what applications are discussed.

Encyclopedia Entry

Write a one- or two-page entry for an encyclopedia of calculus, explaining one of the following: functions, integrals, infinite series, or reflective properties of conic sections.

Historical Vignette

Write a one- to three-paragraph vignette on a mathematician whose work contributed to the topic you're studying. Provide some general-interest biographical details, but focus mainly on this person's impact in the area of study you're discussing.

Poetic Math

Write a poem (limerick or some other form of poetry) explaining some main idea or procedure in calculus.

Dramatic Math

Write a brief dialogue between a teacher and a student discussing the main ideas behind a particular concept or procedure. Examples: finding optimal values of functions; Fundamental Theorem of Calculus; role of Newton and Leibniz in inventing calculus; differentiating compound functions; importance of straight lines for analyzing curves.

Poster Math

Design a poster to illustrate the main ideas, definitions, theorems, techniques, and applications of a topic. Examples: differentiating functions, integrating functions, approximating functions using polynomials, using series for numbers and functions.

This Year in Sports

Compile an accurate and comprehensive manual of sports records and statistics for one school year at your school. Include a statistical comparison of your school's records to the records of one other school in your conference, or to a previous year in your school.

Political Science

Both Sides Now

Write an essay discussing the views of both sides during the emergence of the Cold War in the 1940s and 1950s, explaining how the American view led to the "Truman Doctrine."

Running to Win

Using what you have learned about successful campaigns, choose a state politician running for office and write this person a letter in which you propose a weekend schedule of campaign activities.

Public Policy and Politics

Write an essay examining the history of a public institution (like public education or public health). In your paper, (1) describe the private institutions that were responsible for the particular service before the public system was established and (2) explain how the public establishment affected the private institutions.

Price Supports and People

Research the impact that a U.S. government price-support policy is having on people in a third-world country. For example, how is the policy supporting the production of sugar beets in the U.S. affecting people who raise sugarcane in the Dominican Republic?

NAFTA's Impact

Write an essay examining the role that NAFTA (North American Free Trade Agreement) has played in moving an industry like agriculture, auto production, or textiles out of this country and into places like Mexico, Central America, and South America.

Montesquieu's Theory

In an essay, first describe Montesquieu's theory of a balanced political constitution. Then explain how the theory was implemented in the U.S. Constitution.

Law's History

Write a research paper describing the development of codified law in (1) ancient Mesopotamia, (2) ancient Rome, or (3) Europe during the High Middle Ages. Explain the purpose of law as well as the basis for its authority.

Community-Leader Digest

Develop an informational brochure for publication, featuring profiles of all the elected or appointed leaders in your community.

I Believe!

Write an editorial in which you argue for or against a local law or ordinance.

Psychology

Your Narrative

Write a narrative about how one person affected your life for good or for ill. Describe specific scenes or confrontations and explain how you felt at the time, and how you feel now as you reflect on those experiences.

Interpret Your Dreams

Keep a record of your dreams. Then write a paper describing them, identifying possible patterns, and offering explanations for the dreams' contents.

Who's Laughing?

Select 10 daily comic strips and read them for a two-week period, noting how males and females are portrayed (smart, clumsy, dominant, important, assertive, and so on). Then write a summary of your observations.

Acting Strange

Harmlessly break one or two social rules. (Examples: Wear your shirt backwards. Stand very close to the person talking to you.) Then write a report explaining (1) what you did, (2) how people reacted, and (3) how their reactions made you feel.

Why People Help

Do an informal survey asking people, "Why do you do volunteer work?" Then choose a community program that needs and uses volunteer help. Analyze the form, content, and style of the group's requests for help. Write an essay exploring various ideas for effective appeals for volunteer help.

Brainpower

Using one finger on your right hand, count the number of times in one minute that you can press a single computer key; do the process again using one finger on your left hand. Next, repeat both steps while you recite a well-known poem. Record your findings. Then research how brain hemispheres differ, looking for information that may explain the results of your test. Finally, write a brief report on your study.

Social Work and Sociology

Psychology in Marketing

Go to a local grocery store and note the tastes (free food samples), smells (delis, bakeries), sights (colors, food arrangements, ads), sounds (music played), and organization of products. Then write a report analyzing how these characteristics of the store may affect the customers' shopping decisions.

Nutrition vs. Necessity

With a copy of the new USDA food pyramid to guide you, visit a grocery store and decide which items you would purchase if you had $60 to buy a week's worth of groceries for a family of four, and you had to follow the nutritional guidelines. Write a report about your findings.

Cents vs. Sense

Analyze five or six ads on TV or in print and determine what kinds of food and patterns of eating are promoted in the ads. Then read Wendall Berry's essay "The Pleasures of Eating" (in his book *What Are People For*). Finally, write an essay comparing and contrasting the pleasures advocated in the ads with those advocated in the essay.

Surviving Change

Write an essay on Amish or Mennonite farming communities and their responses to the increasing use of technology in agriculture. How have these communities managed to survive in the midst of change? What does their future in agriculture look like?

Grocery Shopping—a Newcomer's View

Interview a recent immigrant or refugee. Ask about his or her reaction after shopping for the first time in a grocery store in this country. Then write a report in which you (1) describe the person's reactions and (2) explain why the person reacted in that manner.

Language Barrier

Interview a recent immigrant or foreign student who must struggle to communicate clearly in English. Ask what the person finds most challenging, most helpful, most discouraging, and most encouraging about learning the English language. Report your findings in writing.

Different Ages, Different Opinions?

Interview 10 students (5 who are in high school and 5 who are in college) about (1) the number of courses they're taking, (2) the time spent on homework, and (3) the value of the education they're receiving. Then, in an essay, compare and contrast responses from the two groups, identify possible patterns in the responses, and summarize what you learned.

Pardon Me

Develop a 1990s stylebook of etiquette for students in your school. Focus on classroom conduct, group skills, lunchroom manners, boy/girl relationships, and so on.

Implementing a Writing Workshop

In a writing workshop, the primary focus is to provide students with a large block of time to work on writing projects of their choice. At least 30 minutes should be reserved for writing or a writing-related activity such as researching, conferencing, or publishing. Many instructors also reserve time for minilessons (5-10 minutes), status checks to keep track of the students' work (2-3 minutes), and sharing sessions (5 minutes). *Note:* For some minilessons, an instructor might require that all students participate in the work. For other ones, only certain students may be required to participate, depending on the needs of the students and the subject of the minilesson.

> *"The trouble with most school writing is that it is not genuine communication . . . The teacher is seen as an assessor and not as someone interested in being communicated with."*
> —Nancy Martin

Instructor's Role

The instructor serves as a facilitator, making sure that his or her classroom is conducive to writing, conferencing, reading, and researching. He or she also serves as a writing mentor, helping each student make the most out of each writing project.

There's a direct correlation between the effectiveness of a writing workshop and the effectiveness of an instructor's record keeping and planning. A workshop facilitator must make sure that important concepts are covered, essential skills are taught, and each student's progress is charted during the course of each grading period. This can only be accomplished through careful planning and record keeping. Status-of-the-class sheets, daily work charts, conference checklists, and semester evaluation forms are just a few of the many organizers that can help instructors manage a workshop.

Student's Role

Students should come to each workshop session with their writing folders intact, containing all drafts of their works in progress. They should also have a plan of action in mind for each session (that plan should obviously include some form of writing). Students' success or failure in a workshop depends on their ability to manage time effectively and turn the required work in on time. For this reason, they need to be aware of established due dates and deadlines.

The class should also expect to share their writing, offer advice to their writing colleagues, and generally conduct themselves maturely and cooperatively. Finished pieces of writing should reflect a student's best efforts after careful revising, editing, and proofreading. At the end of a grading period, students should compile the required number of finished pieces in a portfolio for evaluation.

Special Note: Below, you will find a basic weekly schedule for a writing workshop. This schedule can serve as a starting point for planning. Individual instructors will definitely want to make adjustments to meet the specific needs in their classrooms.

Weekly Schedule

This schedule can be adjusted to suit individual classes. One instructor may conduct a series of three or four writing workshops for every assignment throughout the semester. Another instructor may vary the regular routine to conduct extended lessons dealing with important writing skills. Still another instructor may schedule the entire semester in six-session blocks, each consisting of five writing workshops followed by a "coffeehouse" during which students read and discuss their writing.

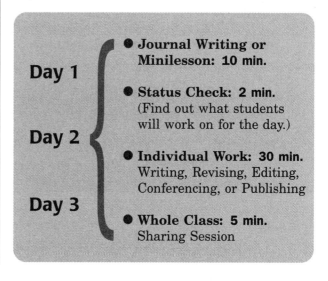

Day 1

● **Journal Writing or Minilesson: 10 min.**

● **Status Check: 2 min.**
(Find out what students will work on for the day.)

Day 2

● **Individual Work: 30 min.**
Writing, Revising, Editing, Conferencing, or Publishing

Day 3

● **Whole Class: 5 min.**
Sharing Session

Evaluating Student Writing

> "If any man wishes to write in a clear style, let him first be clear in his thoughts."
>
> —Johann Wolfgang von Goethe

Instructors need to practice two different types of evaluation when they respond to student writing: **formative evaluation** (evaluating writing in progress) and **summative evaluation** (evaluating the total outcome, or sum, of the student's effort). Formative evaluation does not result in a grade; summative evaluation does. Most instructors give students a set number of points (a performance score) during the formative steps in the writing process.

Formative Evaluation

Formative evaluation is often used for writing-to-learn activities, prewriting activities, writing in progress, journal entries, and so forth. Four types of formative evaluation are widely used:

- Desk-side conference
- Scheduled instructor/student conference
- Written questions and responses
- Peer responses

Note: Make sure your students understand writing as a process. Review "The Writing Process" in the *Write for College* handbook as necessary.

DESK-SIDE CONFERENCES occur when an instructor asks a student questions and makes responses while a student is working. In the early stages of the writing process, responses and questions should be about writing ideas, content, audience, purpose, generating ideas, and getting those ideas on paper. Questions should be open-ended. This gives the writer "space" to talk. When a writer is talking, he or she is thinking, clarifying, and making decisions. Instructors should not attempt to solve problems for the students, but instead ask questions and suggest possible solutions.

Respond to a student's paper as a reader, not as a instructor. Address underdevelopment, the most common problem many writers face in the first stages of the writing process. Also see the PQS conference format discussed in the next column.

SCHEDULED INSTRUCTOR/STUDENT CONFERENCES provide opportunities for students to initiate conferences with you. Student/instructor conferences usually take one of three forms:

- Student-directed conference
- PQS conference
- Small group conference

A **student-directed conference** may occur when a student has finished a rough draft or a final draft, has identified a problem or need, wishes to establish new criteria for his or her next project, or wishes to share a breakthrough, a success, a good thing.

A **PQS conference** (praise-P, question-Q, and suggest-S) will help you refrain from dominating the conference or overteaching. A typical conference lasts from 3 to 5 minutes. First, offer specific and honest praise. Second, ask an appropriate question (one that relates to the writing stage the student is in and prompts student talking). Last, offer one or two suggestions.

A **small group conference** may be a group of three to five students who are at the same stage of the writing process or are experiencing the same problem. The goal of a small group conference is twofold: first, to help students improve their writing and second, to help students develop as evaluators of writing.

HINT: Collect student revising samples. Include before-and-after passages. "Label" these samples and put them in a binder students can refer to whenever they need help with their writing.

> "My predominant impression has been that [writing] is fantastically over-evaluated. Students are graded on everything they do every time they turn around. Grades generate anxiety and hard feelings . . . Common sense suggests that they ought to be reduced to the smallest possible numbers necessary to find out how students are getting along . . . , but teachers keep piling them up like squirrels gathering nuts . . ."
>
> —Paul Diderich, *Measuring Growth in English*

WRITTEN QUESTIONS AND RESPONSES help an instructor vary his or her evaluating techniques, supplement desk-side conferencing, and provide a lasting record.

Collect works in progress. Write comments similar to those you use in conferences and ask open-ended questions so students can actively seek solutions.

In the editing and proofreading stage you can ask, "Why do you need a comma here?" Students must answer the questions and correct the errors. However, with inexperienced writers it is best not to mark all of the errors. Draw a double line to indicate where you stopped marking errors.

Students learn as much from hearing what they are doing right as they do from hearing what they are doing wrong. Make positive comments! Identify good things!

PEER RESPONSES can help students become expert responders, but you must train them. You have already begun to do this in both desk-side and scheduled conferences.

Provide some guide sheets or forms for students to use in peer conferences. It is best if students work in pairs and have a very limited agenda. Always model how to use the form for your entire class. Impose a time limit to keep students on task (15-20 minutes).

One very simple process of peer advising is to ask a student to read his or her partner's paper and then generate three questions beginning with *who, what, where, when, why,* or *how.* The paper and the questions, which serve as a starting point for discussion, are returned to the writer, who responds. You can use more elaborate processes as students become better peer responders. (See "Peer Reviewing" in *Write for College* for more information.)

> *"At first, I thought, 'Why bother?' What did we know about writing? I resented the group discussions about my writing and offered very few suggestions. Later I realized that we were talking about what we each need right now, for this paper. That was something even a teacher couldn't tell me."*
>
> —Paul, a student

Summative Evaluation

Summative evaluation produces a grade and is used for final papers and projects. Once you assign a grade, the student interprets this as a signal that this piece of writing is finished. We want our students to value the learning process as much if not more than the final product, and we want their attention on personal goals, not grades.

However, the day will come when we must assign a grade. Here are some general principles to help you do that:

1. Clearly establish the criteria for each piece of writing or for each student. Limit the criteria so you do not overwhelm the student or yourself. Establishing criteria for each student during a personal conference will allow you to fit the criteria to the student and his/her learning task.

2. Ask students to help you develop the criteria. This can be done in personal conferences or with the whole class. Students readily accept and understand criteria they have helped build.

3. Students must have ample opportunities for formative evaluation before their final product receives a grade. Students deserve points for the work they have done during the writing process.

4. Concern for content, fluency, and fresh ideas should be of primary concern during summative evaluation for young writers. Mechanical correctness will follow fluency. As students gain control of their language, their errors decrease.

5. Students should be involved in the summative evaluation. A form that asks them to circle the best parts of their writing, list the problems they encountered, draw a squiggly line around parts they would work on if they had more time, as well as list the revision suggestions they tried gives students input. In addition to the above information, they should be asked how much time they put into a project and what grade they would give themselves.

6. You will already be familiar with the piece of writing because of the formative evaluations. You may choose one of the systems that follow to establish a grade.

Approaches for Evaluating Writing

Analytic scales establish the features necessary for a successful piece of writing and attribute point values for each feature. The grade derives from the point total. Many students like this form of evaluation because it is concrete, and it highlights specific strengths and weaknesses in their writing. The emphasis of analytic scales tends, however, to be on the parts rather than the whole.

Holistic grading evaluates a piece of writing as a whole. The most basic approach to holistic grading is to read the paper rather quickly for a general impression. The paper is graded according to this impression. A reader might also compare a particular piece with a number of pieces already graded, or grade it for the appearance of elements important to that type of writing. Holistic grading helps instructors reward creativity, inventiveness, and overall effect.

Task-specific scoring accords a grade based on how well a student has accomplished specific rhetorical tasks. An instructor might, for example, create a scoring checklist or guide for a short fiction writing assignment. This checklist would include those elements that are inherent in this writing form—plot, characterization, point of view, etc. Students must understand the criteria for scoring before they begin their writing. This type of grading addresses specific rather than open-ended writing assignments.

Portfolio grading gives students an opportunity to choose pieces of writing to be graded. This is a common method of evaluation in writing workshops. Workshop students compile all of their work in a portfolio or folder. Instructors require them to submit a specified number of finished projects for grading each quarter or semester. Students enjoy this method of evaluation because it gives them some control over the evaluation process; instructors like it because they don't have to grade everything a student has written, and this lessens their workload.

A performance system is a quick and simple method of evaluation. If students complete a writing activity and it meets the previously established level of acceptability, they receive the pre-established grade or points for completing the assignment. The student either has completed the activity or has not. (This method works well for evaluating journals.)

Responding to Student Writing

The following guidelines will help you assess nongraded and graded writing. (Nongraded writing refers to writing in progress and writing-to-learn activities.)

Responding to Nongraded Writing (Formative)

● Discard your red pens and pencils. Use a #2 pencil when responding to student writing.

● Clarify criteria for evaluation. Make the criteria known in advance.

● Scan the writing once quickly. Ask the question, "Has the student understood and responded appropriately to the activity?"

● Reread the writing and indicate that it has or has not fulfilled the requirements of the activity. You may choose to place a check mark on the front page, write a summary sentence on the last page, and/or note areas needing further attention.

● Respond noncritically. Use positive, supportive language.

● Use marginal dialogue. Resist writing on or over the student's writing.

● Underline points you wish to highlight, question, or confirm.

● Whenever possible, respond in the form of questions.

● Encourage risk taking.

Evaluating Graded Writing (Summative)

● Have students submit prewriting and rough drafts with their final drafts.

● Scan a final draft once, focusing on the writing as a whole.

● Read it again, this time evaluating it for its adherence to previously established criteria.

● As you read the draft a second time, make marginal notations. Be sure the notations address the process as you evaluate the product. Use supportive language.

● Scan the writing a third and final time. Write a summary comment on the last page of the student's writing.

● Assign a grade. Remember that you are evaluating both process and product.

Using Writing Portfolios

More and more, English instructors are making portfolios an important part of their writing programs. Will portfolios work for you? Will they help you and your students assess their writing? Read on and find out.

What is a writing portfolio?

A writing portfolio is a limited collection of a student's writing for evaluation. A portfolio is different from the traditional writing folder. A writing folder (also known as a working folder) contains all of a student's work; a portfolio contains only a student's best results.

Why should I ask students to compile writing portfolios?

Having students compile portfolios makes the whole process of writing so much more meaningful to them. They will more willingly put forth their best efforts as they work on various writing projects, knowing that they are accountable for producing a certain number of finished pieces for publication. They will more thoughtfully approach writing as an involved and recursive process of drafting, sharing, and rewriting, knowing that this process leads to more effective writing. And they will more responsibly craft finished pieces, knowing that their final evaluation depends on the finished products they include in their portfolios.

Any or all methods of assessment can be employed when portfolios are used, including self-evaluation, peer evaluation, contract writing, traditional grading, and so on. (For more on assessment, refer to pages 39-41 in this manual.)

How many pieces of writing should be included in a portfolio?

Although you and your students will best be able to decide this, we advise that students compile at least six or seven pieces of writing in a portfolio each semester. (Students could contract for a certain amount of required writing.) All of the drafts should be included for each piece. Students should also be required to include a reflective writing or self-critique sheet that assesses their writing progress.

Special Note: Some instructors allow students to include one or two pieces of writing from other disciplines in their portfolios.

When do portfolios work best?

Students need plenty of class time to work on writing if they are going to produce effective portfolios. If they are used properly, portfolios turn reluctant writers into practicing writers. And practicing writers need regularly scheduled blocks of time to write, think, talk, and explore options in their writing over and over again.

How can I help my students with their portfolio writing?

Allow students to explore topics of genuine interest to them. Also allow them to write for many different purposes and audiences and in many different forms.

In addition, expect students to evaluate their own writing and the writing of their peers as it develops—and help them to do so. (See "Peer Reviewing" in the handbook for help.) Provide them with sound guidance when they need help with a writing problem. And create a classroom environment that encourages students to immerse themselves in writing.

How do I grade a portfolio?

Base each grade on goals you and your students establish at the beginning of the grading period and on what is achieved as evidenced in the portfolio. Many instructors develop a critique sheet for assessment that is based on the goals established by the class. (It's critical that students know how many pieces they should include in their portfolios, how their work should be arranged in their portfolios, how the portfolios will be assessed, and so on.)

"Portfolios have become each student's story of who they are as readers and writers, rich with the evidence of what they are able to do and how they are able to do it."

—Linda Rief, *Seeking Diversity*

The Forms of Writing
Instructor's Notes

Write for College Activities and Outcomes

The activities in the *Write for College* framework provide students with a wide variety of opportunities to re-create and connect past incidents, to analyze processes and information, to develop essays and personal responses, and to form explanations and summaries.

PERSONAL WRITING

Personal Reminiscence	● Re-create a personal experience from the past.
Personal Essay	● Explore a subject of personal interest in a free-flowing essay.
Essay of Experience	● Develop an essay exploring what a personal experience says about you or your society.

REPORT WRITING

Summary Report	● Summarize accurately the contents of a single source of information.
Compiled Report	● Draw information from several sources into a focused report.
Interview Report	● Report the details of an interview with someone who has special knowledge or experiences.
Observation Report	● Base a report on sensory impressions related to a visit.
Personal Research Report	● Present your research findings on a topic of personal interest.

ANALYTICAL WRITING

Analysis of a Process	● Explain how something works in a step-by-step manner.
Essay of Comparison	● Point out the similarities and differences between two subjects.
Essay of Classification	● Create understanding of a whole by exploring its parts.
Essay of Definition	● Define a concept using a variety of approaches.
Cause/Effect Essay	● Speculate upon the causes or effects of a problem.
Problem/Solution Essay	● Propose a solution(s) to a real problem.
Essay of Evaluation	● Assess a policy, topic, class, etc., as to its value or worth.

PERSUASIVE WRITING

Editorial	● Present a strongly felt position about a timely issue.
Personal Commentary	● Present your observations about the state of the world around you in an interesting, colorful style.
Essay of Argumentation	● Argue convincingly for or against a controversial topic.
Position Paper	● Present your position on a significant issue.

WRITING ABOUT LITERATURE

Personal Response	● Form a personal response to a literary work.
Review	● Develop a review suitable for publication.
Limited Literary Analysis	● Prepare a close analysis of one story, theme, character, etc.
Extended Literary Analysis	● Develop an extensive literary analysis displaying a thorough understanding of an author and his or her work.

Implementing the Forms of Writing

The guidelines that follow will help instructors to carry out the framework activities as classwide projects. (In a writing workshop, instructors can assign the frameworks on an individual basis, allowing students to use the writing guidelines and models on their own.)

Planning

1. Gain a clear understanding of the framework activity by previewing the "Instructor's Notes," the writing guidelines, and the related models.

2. Review all of the "Related Workshops" listed in the "Instructor's Notes" for possible inclusion in the activity.

Introducing the Activity

3. Introduce the activity by implementing any combination of the following:
- Ask students to review the writing guidelines.
- Have them read and react to one or more of the writing models.
- Discuss and/or display the "Framing Questions" to help students establish a focus for their work.
- Implement one or more of the "Selecting Activities."
- Offer a related writing prompt for an introductory exploratory writing.

Facilitating the Students' Work

4. Help students carry out their work by doing the following:
- Guide them in their searching, selecting, generating, and writing as outlined in the writing guidelines.
- Provide opportunities for them to write, read, and share in class.
- Consider implementing one of the workshops listed under "Related Workshops."
- Identify relevant handbook pages.

Closing Out the Activity

5. Bring the writing activity to an effective close in one or more of these ways:
- Ask students to conduct peer revising and editing sessions.
- Have them share (and evaluate) finished products.
- Encourage students to submit their work for publication.
- Challenge them to write additional pieces related to this framework.

Instructor's Notes Preview

The "Instructor's Notes" for each framework writing activity offer advice, insights, options, and related activities to help instructors guide and enrich their students' work.

● The opening remarks establish a starting point for planning and implementing.

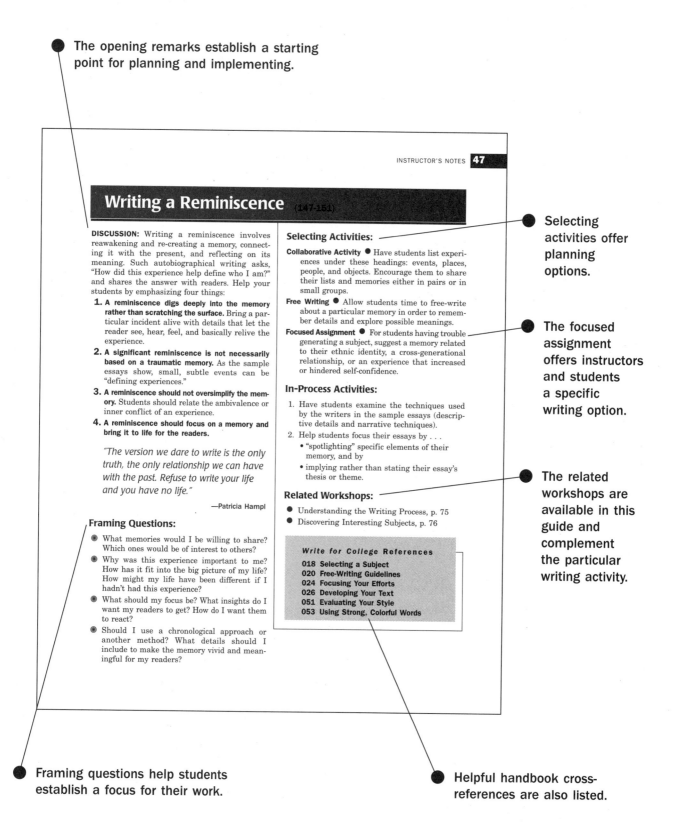

Writing a Reminiscence (147-151)

DISCUSSION: Writing a reminiscence involves reawakening and re-creating a memory, connecting it with the present, and reflecting on its meaning. Such autobiographical writing asks, "How did this experience help define who I am?" and shares the answer with readers. Help your students by emphasizing four things:

1. **A reminiscence digs deeply into the memory rather than scratching the surface.** Bring a particular incident alive with details that let the reader see, hear, feel, and basically relive the experience.

2. **A significant reminiscence is not necessarily based on a traumatic memory.** As the sample essays show, small, subtle events can be "defining experiences."

3. **A reminiscence should not oversimplify the memory.** Students should relate the ambivalence or inner conflict of an experience.

4. **A reminiscence should focus on a memory and bring it to life for the readers.**

"The version we dare to write is the only truth, the only relationship we can have with the past. Refuse to write your life and you have no life."

—Patricia Hampl

Framing Questions:

● What memories would I be willing to share? Which ones would be of interest to others?

● Why was this experience important to me? How has it fit into the big picture of my life? How might my life have been different if I hadn't had this experience?

● What should my focus be? What insights do I want my readers to get? How do I want them to react?

● Should I use a chronological approach or another method? What details should I include to make the memory vivid and meaningful for my readers?

Selecting Activities:

Collaborative Activity ● Have students list experiences under these headings: events, places, people, and objects. Encourage them to share their lists and memories either in pairs or in small groups.

Free Writing ● Allow students time to free-write about a particular memory in order to remember details and explore possible meanings.

Focused Assignment ● For students having trouble generating a subject, suggest a memory related to their ethnic identity, a cross-generational relationship, or an experience that increased or hindered self-confidence.

In-Process Activities:

1. Have students examine the techniques used by the writers in the sample essays (descriptive details and narrative techniques).

2. Help students focus their essays by . . .
   • "spotlighting" specific elements of their memory, and by
   • implying rather than stating their essay's thesis or theme.

Related Workshops:

● Understanding the Writing Process, p. 75
● Discovering Interesting Subjects, p. 76

Write for College References

018 Selecting a Subject
020 Free-Writing Guidelines
024 Focusing Your Efforts
026 Developing Your Text
051 Evaluating Your Style
053 Using Strong, Colorful Words

● Selecting activities offer planning options.

● The focused assignment offers instructors and students a specific writing option.

● The related workshops are available in this guide and complement the particular writing activity.

● Framing questions help students establish a focus for their work.

● Helpful handbook cross-references are also listed.

Writing a Reminiscence

DISCUSSION: Writing a reminiscence involves reawakening and re-creating a memory, connecting it with the present, and reflecting on its meaning. Such autobiographical writing asks, "How did this experience help define who I am?" and shares the answer with readers. Help your students by emphasizing four things:

1. **A reminiscence digs deeply into the memory rather than scratching the surface.** Bring a particular incident alive with details that let the reader see, hear, feel, and basically relive the experience.

2. **A significant reminiscence is not necessarily based on a traumatic memory.** As the sample essays show, small, subtle events can be "defining experiences."

3. **A reminiscence should not oversimplify the memory.** Students should relate the ambivalence or inner conflict of an experience.

4. **A reminiscence should focus on a memory and bring it to life for the readers.**

"The version we dare to write is the only truth, the only relationship we can have with the past. Refuse to write your life and you have no life."

—Patricia Hampl

Framing Questions:

◉ What memories would I be willing to share? Which ones would be of interest to others?

◉ Why was this experience important to me? How has it fit into the big picture of my life? How might my life have been different if I hadn't had this experience?

◉ What should my focus be? What insights do I want my readers to get? How do I want them to react?

◉ Should I use a chronological approach or another method? What details should I include to make the memory vivid and meaningful for my readers?

Selecting Activities:

Collaborative Activity ● Have students list experiences under these headings: events, places, people, and objects. Encourage them to share their lists and memories either in pairs or in small groups.

Free Writing ● Allow students time to free-write about a particular memory in order to remember details and explore possible meanings.

Focused Assignment ● For students having trouble generating a subject, suggest a memory related to their ethnic identity, a cross-generational relationship, or an experience that increased or hindered self-confidence.

In-Process Activities:

1. Have students examine the techniques used by the writers in the sample essays (descriptive details and narrative techniques).

2. Help students focus their essays by . . .
   - "spotlighting" specific elements of their memory, and by
   - implying rather than stating their essay's thesis or theme.

Related Workshops:

● Understanding the Writing Process, p. 75
● Discovering Interesting Subjects, p. 76

Writing a Personal Essay (152-156)

DISCUSSION: As the handbook notes, the personal essay centers on the writer's strong feelings about something related to his or her own life. Students may hesitate to share such feelings, but you can help them by emphasizing the following:

1. **Strong feelings (positive, negative, and mixed) are often connected with change, conflict, and confusion.** Students should start by focusing on experiences that left them with more questions than answers.

2. **The personal essay form allows students to write freely.** They should try to develop their distinctive voices.

3. **The personal essay focuses on not only relating the writer's experiences (like a reminiscence) but also reflecting on them.**

4. **The personal essay presents the writer's experience while inviting readers to reflect on their own lives.** As Alice Walker once said about one of her own essays, it is "a personal account that is yet shared, in its theme and its meaning, by all of us."

"There are many truths of which the full meaning cannot be realized until personal experience has brought it home."
—John Stuart Mill

Framing Questions:

◉ What strong feelings do I have or have I had about an aspect of my life? Which subject do I want to explore and share in writing?

◉ How should I approach my writing? How should I begin? How should I relate my experience? How should I reflect on it?

◉ What main point do I want to make? Is this focus centered on change, conflict, or confusion?

◉ How can my voice come through? What tone can I use?

◉ How do I want my readers to react to my ideas?

Selecting Activities:

Collaborative Activity ● Have students list what they consider to be strong feelings. Then have them connect different experiences (events, people, places, objects) with these feelings. Finally, ask these questions: (1) What kinds of experiences seem related to what kinds of feelings? (2) What causes these feelings and what are their effects? (3) Do these feelings change or remain the same?

Free Writing ● Get students to explore their intense feelings through a writing prompt following this format: "I've been frustrated (or angry, joyful, etc.) because . . . ."

Focused Assignment ● For students having trouble finding a subject, suggest one of the following: styles or fashions, gender relationships, work and play, an experience of injustice.

In-Process Activities:

Help students add depth, honesty, and energy to their writing by considering the following issues in the model essays and in their own work:

1. Have students study how the writers blend the narrative with the analysis. Where do the writers narrate and describe their experiences? Where do they explain and reflect on them? Do they tell or show their strong feelings for the topic?

2. Ask students to explore the depth of the experience. How do the writers show mixed feelings or unresolved conflicts?

3. Have students find the universal in the particular. What patterns do the writers see in their experiences? Are these patterns familiar to readers? What is the underlying truth of each experience?

4. Ask students whether the tone matches the topic: Is the tone appropriate to the experience —light or heavy, comic or serious, a mixture?

Related Workshops:

● Finding a Voice, pp. 82-83
● Pronoun References, pp. 113-114

Write for College **References**

046 Writing with Style
049 Developing a Sense of Style
057 Using an Alternative Style
059 Avoiding Cliches
100 Selecting Supporting Details
101 Arranging Your Details

Writing an Essay of Experience (157-161)

DISCUSSION: "Chalk one up for experience." This proverb captures the spirit of an essay of experience. Here, students reflect upon situations that gave them a new perspective, taught them a lesson, or enriched their lives. Unlike the reminiscence, which simply recalls and records a memory, and the personal essay, which explores the writer's strong feelings, the essay of experience focuses on analyzing and interpreting an experience that was life changing:

1. **The essay centers on perception—developing insight into life-changing experiences.**

2. **These changes can vary from radical shifts in worldview or self-image to subtle changes in understanding or attitude.**

3. **These personal changes can be examined in light of both the experience and any outside social forces.**

4. **An essay about change naturally shapes itself into a before-and-after form, though this form can be used flexibly.** (See the models.)

5. **The essay should both interest and instruct readers.**

"Everyone's life, I suppose, has its demarcation lines—its latitudes and longitudes passing through time. Some of these lines define events that everyone shares—others are confined to personal—even to secret lives."

—Ben Max, narrator in Timothy Findley's "Stones"

Framing Questions:

◉ What major and minor changes have happened in my life? What experiences led to these changes? Which experience interests me most?

◉ What is the meaning of the experience? What do I understand about the change? What do I need to explore further?

◉ How do I want to develop my writing—to present the experience and interpret the change? Should I follow the before-and-after approach?

◉ How do I want readers to react to my experience and insight?

Selecting Activities:

Collaborative Activity ● Examine Klompien's "In the Heart of Green Valley" (003 to 015 in *Write for College*). His piece shows students the process of turning an experience into an essay.

Free Writing ● Have students free-write to generate topics, using the following prompts:
I should have known better when . . .
Before I was . . . , but now I am . . .
The first time that I really understood . . .

Focused Assignment ● Students might consider journeys that expanded their "horizons," or experiences that changed their views of home, neighborhood, or city.

In-Process Activities:

1. Review the model essays, including "In the Heart of Green Valley," exploring the following:
   • Retrospective narrative method: Note how each writer, now more mature, looks back on past ignorance, mistakes, misunderstandings.
   • Organization: Each essay modifies the before-and-after pattern in order to present and analyze the experience.

2. After students have completed their first drafts, have them exchange essays. They should give each other feedback in writing: "Before this experience, you . . . . After this experience, you . . . ."

3. Encourage students to use symbols (objects, people, events) to create a shorthand that deepens a story's meaning (e.g., the food and the miniskirt in Amy Tan's essay). Have students isolate images in their essays and explore ways of discovering their symbolic value.

Related Workshops:

● Searching and Shaping Subjects, pp. 77-78
● Writing in Detail, p. 86

Write for College **References**

003 One Writer's Process
034 Peer Reviewing
046 Writing with Style

Writing a Summary Report (164-165)

DISCUSSION: A summary extracts main ideas from a piece of writing and then shapes that material clearly and coherently. Summarizing helps students (1) sharpen reading and thinking skills, (2) support ideas in essays, (3) write abstracts for research projects, and (4) prepare for workplace summaries of documents and meetings. Students need to see a summary as more than simply skimming an article and copying out some sentences.

1. **Connect the summary with another writing project.** For example, have students summarize an article on the environment for a research paper in that subject area.

2. **Allow students to pursue their own interests, writing summaries aimed at informing each other about topics of mutual interest.**

3. **Share effective summarizing tips by showing students how to . . .**
   - annotate photocopied material.
   - skim material for its purpose, audience, main point, and structure.
   - locate key ideas by looking at paragraphs' topic sentences, concluding sentences, and transitional words.
   - leave out secondary material, such as background information, examples, and unnecessary descriptive details.

Framing Questions:

- Why am I summarizing this material? How brief or detailed should my summary be? Who might use it and why?
- What is the writer's purpose? Who are the intended readers?
- What main point is the writer making?
- What secondary ideas and information support and develop the main idea?
- What is the piece's structure or organization?
- What ideas *don't* I understand in this piece of writing? How can I clarify them?
- How can I put these ideas together clearly and smoothly, in my own words?

Selecting Activities:

Consider these options for making the assignment relevant and manageable:

Collaborative Activities ● Assign a single article or chapter for the whole class, connecting the piece with a project, a visiting speaker, etc. Discuss with students the reason for the selection.

Divide the class into small groups. Assign each group an article or a chapter. Make the assignment collaborative.

Allow students to choose their articles or chapters for summarizing. Provide guidelines on length and types of material.

In-Process Activities:

1. Share examples of summaries in newspaper and magazine articles, textbooks, research abstracts, business reports, meeting minutes. Have students discuss the purpose and usefulness of summaries.

2. Provide a copy (overhead) of the "Superkids" chapter from *Growing Up Poor* summarized by Julie Ewers (165 in the handbook). Have students compare and contrast the original material to the summary.

3. Review "Writing a Summary" (496-498) with students. Then give them the opportunity to free-write a personal summary of the article they are reading.

4. Let students work on improving the coherence of their rough drafts by reviewing "Transition and Linking Words" (108).

Related Workshops:

- Supporting Your Points, p. 87
- Creating Connections, p. 89

Write for College **References**
108 Connecting Your Details
496 Writing a Summary
500 Writing an Abstract

Writing a Compiled Report (166-170)

DISCUSSION: A compiled report presents readers with carefully integrated and focused information from a number of sources. Compiling involves two tasks: (1) tapping a variety of sources, and (2) making sense out of them.

1. **Students should choose a subject that is current, focused, and interesting to them.**
2. **Students should think of a compiled report as a summary of the available knowledge on a subject.** Therefore, they should seek out a rich variety of credible sources that complement and contrast each other.
3. **Students should focus their reports around their conclusions about the material's meaning.**
4. **Unlike the traditional research paper, the compiled report does not involve formulating an original thesis and developing a lengthy argument in its support.**

Framing Questions:

◉ What current subject do I want to know more about?

◉ How can I narrow my subject so that it's manageable?

◉ What sources of information related to my subject are available? Where can I get a range of perspectives? How can I access the information I need?

◉ What can I expect to gain from investigating this subject? What do I hope to give my readers?

◉ Where does my information lead me—to what conclusion about this subject?

◉ What strategies can I use for developing this focus, organizing the information, and weaving sources together smoothly?

Selecting Activities:

Preliminary Reading ● Send students to newspapers, current events magazines, and textbooks in other courses in order to develop a list of topics they might be interested in researching.

Narrowing the Topic ● Encourage students to narrow their topic by using clustering to find a focus.

Focusing the Research ● Direct students to brainstorm for questions they want to answer about their topic.

Checking for Sources ● Encourage students to consider a variety of information sources, both primary and secondary. Consider linking this research with library orientation and instruction in keyword searching.

Focused Assignment ● For students who have problems selecting a subject, suggest a recent development in technology, popular culture, the environment, or the arts.

In-Process Activities:

1. Review the handbook models to check out the writers' conclusions, variety of sources used, integration of sources, and methods of creating reader interest.
2. Help students work with sources by practicing on a newspaper or magazine article: give each student a copy of an article; read it aloud; let students reread it and pull out the main ideas and key concepts; together, create a master list of possible sources on the board or overhead; and let students write a summary of the piece.
3. Assist students in coming to conclusions about the information they've gathered through focused free writing on (a) the connections and (b) the contrasts between their sources.

Related Workshops:

● Devising a Writing Plan, p. 80
● Advising in Peer Groups, p. 96

Write for College References

100 Selecting Supporting Details
286 Steps in the Process (research paper)
294 Writing Responsibly
300 MLA Documentation Style
444 Searching for Information
456 Using Electronic Sources
496 Writing a Summary
541 Conducting Interviews

Writing an Interview Report (171-175)

DISCUSSION: When carefully planned and executed, the interview report allows students to conduct primary research and share another person's story. Help students by emphasizing the following:

1. The choice of an interview subject is crucial. Explore with students how interview subjects fall naturally into two categories: experts on a subject and people who have had a special experience.

2. A strong interview report grows out of effective interview questions. The students' questions imply a focus for their reports.

3. For an effective interview, students need to follow the process—from exploring the subject's background to writing a follow-up thank-you note.

4. Interviews are often part of larger projects. If possible, connect the interview report with a research paper that students are working on.

"The chief reward of [interviewing] is the joy of learning, of coming away from each person with a wider angle of vision on the time I live in. . . ." —Bill Moyers

Framing Questions:

- Do I know someone I want to interview? An expert? What person do I know who has had unique experiences?
- What do I know about the subject and the person? Where can I look up more information about him or her, or about the topic?
- What can and can't this person tell me?
- What questions do I want to ask?
- What details must I take care of to set up and do the interview?
- How do I want to shape and share the report?

Selecting Activities:

Warm-Up ● Give students an opportunity to browse through magazines and newspapers for interviews or to look through books or other collections of interviews. Ask them to consider the types of people who get interviewed and the types of questions they get asked.

Collaborative Activity ● Let students brainstorm lists of people either who are experts in a subject or who have had special experiences. Students may also brainstorm lists of issues or topics they find interesting in the community. Give them time to match up topics with people to interview.

Focused Assignment ● Push students to step outside their comfort zones by focusing on "differences"—people coming from different ethnic groups, working in unusual careers, belonging to different socioeconomic groups.

In-Process Activities:

1. Use "Conducting Interviews" (541-542) as a resource. Let students practice drafting questions for various people. Explore how the questions create a focus, and why the differences between open-ended and closed or slanted and neutral questions are important.

2. Review the model interview reports in the handbook and discuss organization options: (a) combining background, paraphrase, summary, and quotation in interview "sections"; (b) giving the interview in a straight transcript form. Have students consider which form will bring their interviewee's story to life.

3. Invite students to share first drafts of their interview reports, and let them complete this prompt: "This interview report taught me . . ."

Related Workshops:

- Logical Organization, p. 88
- Achieving Economy, p. 94

Write for College **References**

019 Selecting a Subject (Essentials of Life Checklist)
050 Writing with a Plan in Mind
541 Conducting Interviews

Writing an Observation Report (176-180)

DISCUSSION: An observation report takes readers inside the writer's experience of a place or an event. Help your students develop their observation skills by stressing the following:

1. Observing should be active, not passive. Students should work on stretching all five of their senses in the act of observation.

2. The observer can never be purely objective. Observation activates the senses, mind, and heart—engaging emotions, reason, and imagination. Saturated with impressions, observers become filters for experiences.

3. Observation reports aim to make the unfamiliar familiar or the familiar fresh. Taking the reader inside the experience involves detailed and suggestive description, carefully chosen comparisons, and focused reflection on the experience's impact and meaning.

4. Strong observation reports often take both writers and readers out of their comfort zones.

Framing Questions:

◉ What place or event would be interesting to observe? Why?

◉ How can I go about recording sensory impressions (sights, sounds, smells, tastes, touches)? How will I position myself as an observer?

◉ How should I present my observations? As a continuous flow of impressions, or in a more structured format?

◉ How should I place myself in the writing?

Selecting Activities:

Collaborative Activity ● Have students brainstorm two lists: (1) places and events that are familiar or comfortable; (2) places and events that are unfamiliar or uncomfortable. Let them share their lists, and then discuss the different observation strategies needed for comfortable and uncomfortable experiences.

Focused Assignment ● Suggest any public location that provides students with a slice of life—a mall, market, coffee shop, post office, library, sports event, etc.

In-Process Activities:

1. Give students a feel for recording sensory observations by playing a 10- to 15-minute videotape of a busy location, or by actually visiting such a place, recording the sights and sounds together. Discuss both the actual sensations and the broader impressions (thoughts, feelings). Remind students that a videotape leaves out taste, touch, and smell.

2. Explore the models in the handbook, pointing out the following:

   • The observations take both writers out of their comfort zones.

   • The writers keep the focus on the experience but also reveal their own presence as observers.

   • Both writers put the observation in context, provide rich sensory details, use comparisons, and reflect on the experience.

Consider sharing bits of effective observation from your favorite writers (e.g., Annie Dillard or Barry Lopez). Invite students to find well-made observations in books and magazines of their choice.

Related Workshops:

● Finding a Form, p. 81
● Parallel Structure, p. 84

***Write for College* References**

018 Selecting a Subject
050 Writing with a Plan in Mind
052 Special Features of Style
053 Using Strong, Colorful Words
057 Using an Alternative Style

Writing a Personal Research Report (181-186)

DISCUSSION: As the name suggests, the personal research report combines elements of personal and report writing by presenting the writer's experience of researching a personally important topic. The skills students learned in exploring experiences, remembering, interviewing, and observing will be useful here. Note the following features of the personal research report:

1. **Students should approach it as a research quest.** The topic must be personally important, one rooted in a deep curiosity or concern.

2. **As much as possible, research should be primary—experiences, memories, observations, interviews, surveys, even experiments.** Traditional library research may supplement this primary research.

3. **The report should focus on the research journey, pointing out discoveries made along the way.**

"Where there is curiosity, a mouse may be caught." —Lu Po Hua

Framing Questions:

⦿ What have I always been curious or concerned about? What am I interested in right now? What knowledge would help me in the future?

⦿ How is my chosen topic of personal relevance?

⦿ What research strategy should I follow to explore this topic? Is researching this topic within my abilities, scope, and time frame?

⦿ What do I already know about this topic?

⦿ Can I do firsthand research on this topic?

⦿ What do I hope to find out?

⦿ How should I present my research journey and share my discoveries?

Selecting Activities:

Free Writing ● Use a prompt to get students thinking about what they find important:

"I always wanted to know . . ."

"I am concerned about . . ."

"In a few years, I will be . . ."

"I think that it's crazy (great, fascinating, foolish, etc.) that . . ."

Focused Assignment ● Follow the lead of the handbook models by suggesting the following topics:

(a) an illness, fear, disability, social attitude, weakness, memory, or loss that has affected the student's life or development

(b) an element of local history—the origins, development, and future of the student's neighborhood, city, or rural area

In-Process Activities:

1. Explore differences between the personal research report and the traditional research paper by reviewing "Research Update" (285). Help students see the value of a research journal—a place where they can keep notes on their investigative journeys and the questions, mysteries, and insights they are exploring.

2. Review the handbook models and discuss why the writers researched their topics, what they did, and what they discovered.

Related Workshops:

● Improving Openings, pp. 91-92
● Improving Focus, p. 100

Write for College References

018 Selecting a Subject
021 Shaping a Subject
024 Focusing Your Efforts
285 Research Update
286 Steps in the Process
444 Searching for Information
541 Conducting Interviews

Writing an Analysis of a Process (189-192)

DISCUSSION: A process is a sequence of events that leads to a specific outcome—a drama, so to speak. Processes make up the fabric of daily life—from people buying groceries to leaves growing and dying to students writing college papers. Help students analyze processes effectively by emphasizing the following:

1. A process analysis can focus on how to do something (instructions), how something works (operation), or how something develops or happens (natural phenomena).

2. An analysis provides an overview of the process and points to the outcome; it also breaks down the process and shows links between the various stages.

3. By vividly and accurately exploring the process, the writer develops an expertise to be shared with readers.

"Writing has been for a long time my major tool for self-instruction and self-development." —Toni Cade Bambara

Framing Questions:

● What processes am I an "expert" in? What processes am I curious about?

● What is the outcome or goal of the process I've chosen?

● What are the main steps and the substeps in the process?

● How do I want to shape my process analysis—as instructions for the reader, or as a process to understand?

● How can I help the reader "see" the process?

● What tone would work best here—light or serious? Should I be present in the analysis, or should I remain in the background?

Selecting Activities:

Collaborative Activities ● Have students turn to the "Essentials of Life Checklist" (019) and brainstorm processes related to a variety of the items. You may also choose to have students brainstorm lists of topics under these headings: (1) Subjects I've Got Some Expertise In and (2) Subjects I'm Curious About, but Don't Fully Understand. Then ask students to cluster processes related to three of the topics.

In-Process Activities:

1. Show students a process happening (perhaps on videotape). Repeat the process, and have students map out the stages using the "Process Analysis" graphic organizer (220) as a guide.

2. Suggest the following mapping options:
   - design a flowchart
   - create a table with these headings: Step #, Action/Development, Relationship to Other Steps and to Outcome, Tools/Materials Needed
   - outline dramatic concepts of plot (beginning, middle, climax, end)

3. Remind students to keep focused as they draft and revise their process analysis by (a) thinking about their readers and (b) getting at the heart of the process.
   - What would the readers already know? What questions would readers have about the process?
   - What is the heart of the process—the outcome, goal, or climactic moment? How can that heart be the focus of the analysis?

4. Help students write coherently by reviewing transitions that show time (108).

Related Workshops:

● Unifying Tone, p. 93
● Evaluating Style, p. 97

Write for College References

018 Selecting a Subject
021 Shaping a Subject
050 Writing with a Plan in Mind
102 Chronological Order
108 Connecting Your Details
110 Mastering the College Essay
220 Using Graphic Organizers

Writing an Essay of Comparison (193-197)

DISCUSSION: Comparing and contrasting means exploring the similarities and differences between two things—holding them up side by side, weighing them and balancing them in order to arrive at some insight into both. Here are key points to help your students perform an effective balancing act:

1. **The topics compared must be compatible—have a logical connecting point, a basis for comparison.** They cannot be two different types of things, nor can one simply be an example of the other.

2. **An in-depth comparison requires a limited focus.**

3. **A rich comparison creates insights by exploring degrees of similarity and difference.** It interprets as well as describes the similarities and differences.

4. **Writers should develop the essay of comparison for a specific purpose by carefully choosing points to compare, giving roughly equal weight to both topics, and choosing whether to emphasize similarities or differences.**

Framing Questions:

◉ What two people, objects, places, experiences, events, or concepts would I like to compare and contrast? Why do I want to compare these topics?

◉ Can these topics be compared? What's the link, the basis of comparison?

◉ What do I already know about each element? What do I need to research?

◉ What elements or aspects of each can I compare? How are the topics similar and different with respect to each point of comparison?

◉ How should I develop and organize the comparison? Given my focus and purpose, how should I balance similarities and differences?

Selecting Activities:

Collaborative Activities ● Have students brainstorm topics on blank paper, one sheet per heading: (1) ideas, concepts, and principles; (2) events and experiences; (3) objects; (4) places; (5) people; (6) works of art, (7) texts; etc. Then have students draw lines between items with obvious connections (similarities and differences); ask them to list the connections.

In groups, let students test their comparison choices: Can the two things actually be compared? Is the comparison narrowly focused? Will a comparison of these things be fruitful? Is information available for the comparison?

Focused Assignment ● Have students compare two types of institutions, such as homes, schools, or places of worship; or ask them to compare two family sitcoms, one from the past and the other from the present.

In-Process Activities:

1. Give students practice in making comparisons. For example, you could bring incandescent and compact fluorescent lightbulbs to class, let students explore similarities and differences, and then hand out *Consumer Reports* articles comparing the bulbs.

2. Examine the comparison models in *Write for College* for (a) the basis of comparison, (b) elements compared, (c) balance, (d) combination of description and interpretation, (e) purpose, and (f) insights gained.

3. Have students explore organization options as they draft: topic by topic, whole versus whole, or all similarities and all differences. They can experiment to discover which options suit their essays.

4. Point students to "Transition and Linking Words" (108) for words used to compare and contrast.

Related Workshops:

● Evaluating Writing, p. 98
● Using Adverb Clauses, p. 102

Writing an Essay of Classification (198-202)

DISCUSSION: Classifying organizes and clarifies knowledge by grouping things based on similarities and differences (e.g., grocery store aisles, bookstore shelves, filing systems, literary genres). The essay of classification, then, takes what is scattered or all mixed together, discovers patterns or categories, and creates a framework for understanding. Here are some key features:

1. **Different principles of grouping create different understandings of the material.** For example, different classification schemes for cars could include *use, horsepower, weight, size, image.*

2. **Whatever the scheme created, the categories should be consistent and complete—based on a careful analysis of the topic.**

3. **The purpose of the classification helps to determine the kind of grouping needed.** Whether giving the big picture or putting elements in a larger context, classification makes sense of information.

4. **A good classification scheme doesn't isolate items within categories.** It shows the connections between the example items (parts) and the whole.

Framing Questions:

◉ What group of people, practices, ideas, and so on am I interested in classifying?

◉ Is my chosen topic focused enough for in-depth analysis?

◉ What's the point of my classification? What purpose does it serve?

◉ How can my goal help me develop consistent and complete categories?

◉ How can I make my essay insightful and interesting for my readers?

Selecting Activities:

Collaborative Activities ● Point students to the "Essentials of Life Checklist" (itself a classification scheme, 019) as a starting point for generating topics. After a brainstorming session, encourage them to use clustering (018) as a strategy for breaking a topic down into categories.

Review and discuss the Library of Congress classification system (448-450)—what it is, how it works, why it's useful. Then have students use the Library of Congress subject headings to explore how possible topics fit into a larger scheme and divide into subtopics.

Free Writing ● Students might free-write about a possible topic by completing this statement: "This topic can be classified by . . . "

Focused Assignment ● Students could focus on college life—types of students, courses, tests, instructors, assignments, social activities.

In-Process Activities:

1. Bring in objects (e.g., building blocks) for students to group according to similarities and differences. Discuss the various principles they come up with. Which groupings prove most useful and understandable?

2. Ask students to find classification schemes in different places, particularly in their textbooks. Have them share the logic of the schemes they've found.

3. Explore the handbook's classification essays by considering (a) personal purpose (value for writer), (b) public purpose (value for reader), (c) the classification principle at work, (d) strategies used to develop consistent and complete categories, (e) the scheme's complexity, (f) the rationale for the method of organization.

4. Point students to the "Classification" graphic organizer (220) as a tool for exploring options for their topics.

Related Workshops:

● Experimenting with Form, p. 85
● Improving Diction, p. 95

Write for College References

018 **Selecting a Subject**
021 **Shaping a Subject**
050 **Writing with a Plan in Mind**
101 **Classification**
110 **Mastering the College Essay**
220 **Using Graphic Organizers**
448 **Classification Systems**
450 **Using the Library of Congress Classification System**

Writing an Essay of Definition

DISCUSSION: The essay of definition probes the significance of a difficult concept, idea, or ideal and shares that deeper understanding with its readers. Help students probe and clarify by stressing the following:

1. **A definition essay can be objective, seeking to get at a term's "essence."** But a definition can also explore the term's relevance for the writer—a personal connection or fascination. With either method, the writer seeks to broaden the reader's comprehension of the term.

2. **A definition essay often has a two-part structure.** An opening creates a focus, generates interest, and provides a sentence definition. A body develops and extends the definition by exploring the parts of the sentence definition, offering facts, examples, anecdotes, quotations, explanations, and comparisons; by tracing the word's origin; or by stating what the term is not—its opposite.

" 'When I use a word,' Humpty Dumpty said, in rather a scornful tone, 'it means just what I choose it to mean—neither more nor less.' "

—Lewis Carroll, *Through the Looking Glass*

Framing Questions:

◉ What concept, idea, or ideal interests me or relates to my experience? Why do I want to probe its meaning?

◉ What are my initial thoughts and feelings about the term? Do I need to go beyond my own knowledge and experience? Where would I find material?

◉ Is the term complex enough for the assignment? What is the term's importance? What are the challenges of understanding this term?

◉ What larger class does the term belong to? What are the term's distinguishing features?

◉ What approach—tone and attitude—should I take in the essay? What will readers gain from this definition?

Selecting Activities:

Collaborative Activities ● Pointing students to the "Essentials of Life Checklist" and the guidelines for free writing and clustering (018-020),

have them list concepts important to their own lives and related to their own curiosity.

Have students share their choices with classmates, getting feedback on interest level, the term's complexity, possible ways of researching the term, and methods of developing the definition.

Focused Assignment ● Have students define a term at the heart of their college experience or definitive of a community they belong to.

In-Process Activities:

1. Explore the handbook models for the connection between the concept and the writer's life, the way the term is used, and the strategies used to develop the definition.

2. Challenge students to capture their term in a single-sentence formal definition using this equation:

   term = larger class + distinguishing features

3. Encourage students to develop their definitions through personal and traditional research:

   • Reflect on the relationship between personal experiences and the term.

   • Ask writing peers to free-write about the term to see what comes to mind for them.

   • Use the "Definition" graphic organizer (221).

   • Question the concept (022).

   • Reflect on what readers would and would not know about the term.

   • Research general and specialized dictionaries, thesauruses, and writings by experts.

Related Workshops:

● Adding Energy and Originality, p. 99
● Clarity, p. 104

Write for College **References**

018 **Selecting a Subject**
021 **Shaping a Subject**
022 **Asking Questions** (concepts)
050 **Writing with a Plan in Mind**
107 **Definition**
110 **Mastering the College Essay**
220 **Using Graphic Organizers**
513 **Building a College-Sized Vocabulary**

Writing a Cause/Effect Essay (207-210)

DISCUSSION: The cause/effect essay explores causal links within a chain of events, developments, or conditions. Students probe their topics by asking "Why?" and testing out "because" answers. Here are some ideas for helping students with this challenging thinking and writing task:

1. **Cause/effect writing traces the links in the chain in either of two directions:**
   - forward from an initiating action to its various results
   - backward from an event or a condition to its possible causes

2. **The writer must develop and support sound logical relationships by detailing the causal connections and considering any outside forces at work in the situation.**

3. **A strong essay addresses cause/effect complexities.** Causes can be immediate or remote, root or perpetuating, obvious or hidden. Effects can be specific or wide-ranging, simple or complex, short-term or long-term, superficial or serious. Causes and effects can be easily confused; moreover, events can seem causally related without being so.

Framing Questions:

- ◉ What event, development, or condition am I curious about? What causal connection or chain reaction would I like to explore? Why?
- ◉ Do I want to trace the range of effects from a specific cause or speculate on the possible causes of a specific effect?
- ◉ What are the actual causal connections at work? How can I discover them, research them, support them, clarify them?
- ◉ What do I want to gain from this analysis? What do I want my readers to understand?
- ◉ How should I organize and present the cause/effect chain reaction?

Selecting Activities:

Collaborative Activity ● Have groups of students brainstorm a list of trends they've noticed, speculate on the causes behind and the effects of one such trend, and then decide which causes are most plausible and which effects most important.

Free Writing ● Let students explore their topics by writing out and exploring "Why?" questions. Begin by listing these broad topics on the board or overhead: workplace, college, personal life, politics, the environment, products and services, life stages, the arts.

Clustering ● Have students choose a cause (an event, a development, or a condition) that they are familiar with or curious about. Then let them cluster all possible results growing out of this cause.

Focused Assignment ● Have students focus on the popularity of an event, activity, person, or place on their campus or in their community.

In-Process Activities:

1. Explore the handbook essays for the (a) writers' motivation, (b) difference between effective and faulty cause/effect thinking, (c) sources of information, and (d) methods of organization. Have students map out the cause/effect chain reactions.

2. Encourage students to research cause/effect connections through a variety of sources: personal experience, analysis and experiment, observations and interviews, articles and books.

3. Challenge students to experiment with organizing and clarifying their cause/effect links: (a) Will they move from cause to effects or from effect to possible causes? (b) How will they introduce the subject? (c) How will they develop causal connections in a logical order and support their arguments with evidence?

Related Workshops:

- ● Crafting Sentences, p. 101
- ● Proofreading: Commas and Semicolons, pp. 121-122

Write for College References

- **018 Selecting a Subject**
- **021 Shaping a Subject**
- **050 Writing with a Plan in Mind**
- **105 Cause and Effect**
- **110 Mastering the College Essay**
- **220 Using Graphic Organizers**

Writing a Problem/Solution Essay (211-215)

DISCUSSION: Like a cause/effect essay, the problem/solution essay explores a causal chain reaction; however, it seeks to break a chain linked to a frustrating or harmful situation. This essay assignment helps students to identify problems and take responsibility for solutions. It prepares them to write proposals that lead to productive changes (in the workplace, government, and elsewhere). Here are some key points for developing sound problem/solution essays:

1. **The writer must explore a real problem—demonstrating a concrete, detailed, and personal understanding of it.**

2. **The solution should be creative, reasonable, and well supported—attacking the problem's root causes.** (No bandages allowed!)

3. **The essay's structure is simple: describe the problem, offer a solution (the thesis), and defend the solution.** Deciding how to combine and balance these elements, however, is complex. Should the problem be simply described or carefully explicated? Should the readers be given a solution or called to action?

4. **The tone the writer uses should fit the seriousness of the problem.**

"A problem well defined is a problem half solved."
　　　　　　　　　　　　　　　　　—Proverb

Framing Questions:

◉ What problem do I want to write about? Why?

◉ What is the nature of this problem—its parts, history, causes, effects, larger context? Do I know of any comparisons for it, examples of it?

◉ What do I know about the problem, and what do I need to research?

◉ Is this a solvable problem?

◉ What are some solutions that get at root causes or counter major effects of the problem?

◉ Should I, and how can I, encourage the readers' ownership of the problem and solution?

◉ What tone should I adopt?

Selecting Activities:

Collaborative Activity ● Allow students to generate ideas with these prompts:

- List groups to which you belong. Brainstorm problems specific to each group.
- Consider situations in which you see a gap between what *should be* and *what is*.
- Consider situations in which you see real or potential danger or injustice.

Focused Assignment ● Students may focus on problems related to gender relationships or money.

In-Process Activities:

1. Students can explore problems and solutions in the following ways:
   - Use "Asking Questions" (022), the "5 W's of Writing" (021), and the "Problem/Solution" graphic organizer (221).
   - Create a dialogue between someone affected by the problem and someone who doesn't think the problem is serious or real.
   - Do primary research (observation, interview, survey, experiment) to gain personal insights.
   - Do secondary research (books, articles) to find background, facts, examples, authoritative opinions, and opposition.

2. Encourage feedback sessions during drafting and revising, asking students to do the following:
   - Read a classmate's problem/solution essay and offer "yes, but" responses to "the problem" and "the solution."
   - Draft two "pay attention!" introductions and get feedback on which one works best. (See 117-118 in *Write for College*.)

Related Workshops:

● Complex Sentences, p. 105
● Parallel Structure, p. 109

Write for College References
018 Selecting a Subject
021 Shaping a Subject
022 Asking Questions
050 Writing with a Plan in Mind
110 Mastering the College Essay
220 Using Graphic Organizers

Writing an Essay of Evaluation (218-219)

DISCUSSION: Evaluation builds on other analytical skills—cause/effect, comparison, definition, classification. Without such a foundation, evaluation may be shaky opinion rather than solid judgment. As a thinking and writing skill used in college courses, work situations, and consumer purchases, evaluation is crucial to students' lives. By using standards to measure the significance of a topic, students sharpen their judgment skills in the evaluation essay. Here are some key points:

1. **Writers must become limited experts on their topic in order to discover the proper criteria for their evaluation process, arrive at a solid judgment, and support that judgment.**

2. **Writers may take a variety of approaches (objective or personal, positive or negative), but the goal is to present a reasonable and fair evaluation of the topic.**

Framing Questions:

◉ What do I want to evaluate? Why?

◉ What are my initial thoughts, feelings, and attitudes toward this topic? How does this topic affect me and others?

◉ What criteria (standards) should I use to make my judgments? How can I weigh my criteria?

◉ What research should I do in order to become an expert on this topic—what rereading, reviewing, revisiting?

◉ What strategies could I use for developing and supporting my evaluation?

◉ What tone should I use—witty, serious, enthusiastic, objective, personal?

Selecting Activities:

Warm-Up ● Have students watch or listen to a show, short film, one-act play, concert, or CD and evaluate the "performance." On what basis do they make their judgments? What evidence do they use to support their views? Where do criteria for judgment come from? What's the difference between an opinion and an expert judgment?

Free Writing ● Use the following free-writing prompts:

"Participating in or witnessing _____ was important to me because . . ."

"We shouldn't ignore _____ because . . ."

Focused Assignment ● Focus the class's work on one subject—films, for example. Together, the class could develop expertise on that one subject, learn criteria used by professional critics, and evaluate specific films.

In-Process Activities:

1. Ask students to study the handbook models and gather book, film, TV show, or product reviews from magazines. Then have them explore (a) the writer's connection with the topic, (b) the evaluation's usefulness to the reader, (c) the evaluative language used, (d) the basis of the judgment, and (e) the research strategies used.

2. Suggest these research strategies:

   • Primary research—personal reflection, rereading, reviewing, revisiting

   • Secondary research—where the topic comes from, what it's part of, what type of topic it is, who created it, who's affected by it, what its history is, and so on

3. Direct students to carefully select criteria for making their judgment. Consider the following writing prompt: "I believe that _____ (topic) is a good/poor _____ because . . ."

Related Workshops:

● Sentence Fragments, p. 103
● Relative Clauses, pp. 107-108

Write for College **References**

018 Selecting a Subject
021 Shaping a Subject
050 Writing with a Plan in Mind
100 Selecting Supporting Details
110 Mastering the College Essay
220 Using Graphic Organizers
256 Writing a Review

Writing an Editorial

DISCUSSION: In editorials, writers add their nickel's worth to a public discussion on a current issue—aiming to raise the awareness or change the minds of readers. For students, the editorial refines thinking skills as they participate in public discourse, building their awareness of current events and their right to respond. They join the press, becoming, in Douglas Cater's phrase, the fourth branch of government. Here are key features of the editorial:

1. **Writers must consider the publication and its readers (the rhetorical situation) in order to "target" their editorials.**

2. **The editorial offers a thoughtful but boldly stated opinion supported with solid evidence and reasoning.**

3. **Restricted to about 750 to 900 words, editorials must get to the point.** Paragraphs and sentences should be short and the writing style concrete. The piece should open with a "lead" that grabs attention, follow with a balanced argument, and close with energy.

4. **Good editorials enhance social dialogue by focusing on a current issue, narrowing the topic, and stating a clear position.**

5. **Students should avoid writing editorials that simply offer an unresearched opinion, or merely sound off.** Editorials should maintain or raise the levels of intelligence, civility, and commitment in public discourse.

Framing Questions:

◉ What current issue of public discussion am I interested in? How does it relate to me or to my community?

◉ What, exactly, is the debate about? What are my initial thoughts and feelings on this issue?

◉ What recent events are related to this topic?

◉ What initial claim or point do I wish to make? How can I support it—with what evidence and reasoning? What are the opposing arguments?

◉ What do I already know about the issue, and what do I need to research?

◉ What audience am I writing for? How can I raise the readers' awareness or change their minds?

◉ How can I open with an effective lead, organize a logical argument, and close with energy?

Selecting Activities:

Collaborative Activity ● Find and copy a newspaper or magazine article on an event that interests your students. In groups, have them explore the issue behind the event, different perspectives on the issue, and possible positions that could be supported in an editorial.

Warm-Up ● Have students read the campus paper, local newspaper, national papers, and weekly newsmagazines. Ask them to copy two articles that sparked their interest and respond to this prompt: "What's the issue? Who should care, and why?"

Brainstorming ● Have students list communities they belong to: dorm, friends, college, generation, family, hometown, state, country, race or ethnic group, and so on. Then let students brainstorm each community's current events, central issues, and publications.

In-Process Activities:

1. Ask students to bring in several editorials. In groups, let them debate each editorial's issue and explore its purpose, claim, tone, support, lead, and ending.

2. Point students to "Thinking Through an Argument" (244-246) for help with developing and supporting their theses. They could refer to that section when testing and sharing their first drafts.

3. Assign students to write three different leads and share them with classmates for feedback. (Leads often determine whether editors will publish and readers will read editorials.)

Related Workshops:

● Supporting Your Points, p. 87
● Traits of an Effective Style, p. 90

Write for College **References**

018 **Selecting a Subject**
021 **Shaping a Subject**
047 **Key Stylistic Reminders**
050 **Writing with a Plan in Mind**
060 **Using Clear, Fair Language**
244 **Thinking Through an Argument**

Writing a Personal Commentary (227-231)

DISCUSSION: Like the editorial, the personal commentary allows students to join the public dialogue about current issues. However, while the editorial offers a boldly stated opinion in response to a current issue, the personal commentary reflects on an ongoing issue of daily life.

1. The personal commentary is exploratory. In it, writers open their window on the world—exploring strong feelings, revising them, and taking a stand. Through curiosity, writers trace the connections between themselves and other people, communities, and issues. The commentary gives writers a chance to say, "This is the way I see the world."

2. The personal commentary is rhetorical. Writers invite readers to say, "I hadn't seen this issue that way." Personal reflection often responds to and sometimes counters popular opinion.

"The life which is unexamined is not worth living."   —Plato

Framing Questions:

◉ What issue connecting my own life with that of others do I want to explore?

◉ How does this topic relate to my experiences, values, and worldview? How can exploring this topic help me see the world more clearly?

◉ What, exactly, is the issue? What do I know about it? What do I need to explore?

◉ What community of readers will I address? How will my perspective relate to their opinions? What tone should I adopt?

◉ How can I focus, develop, and support my commentary? How can I bring it to life?

Selecting Activities:

Free Writing ● Have students read a news article and free-write their personal responses. Then share and discuss their responses, getting at the issues behind the news event and its relationship to individual and community life. Encourage students to perform the same type of free writing with other news stories as a way of discovering commentary topics.

Personal Responses ● Help students explore connections between their lives and current issues in the following ways:

• Have students free-write using the prompt "What's on my mind and in my heart?"

• Have students list major experiences they've had during the past year and explore how those experiences relate to personal, community, and life issues.

• Have students record a week's worth of daily activities in a journal and reflect on the connecting threads between those activities and broader issues.

Focused Assignment ● Offer students one of these topic options: the reality versus the appearance of a place (e.g., campus, hometown); the brave new world of the Internet; his or her relationship to a specific law, rule, or expectation.

In-Process Activities:

1. Explore the handbook models and models from news sources, keeping these issues in mind: (a) the commentary's topic and connection to news stories, (b) the importance of the piece for the writer, (c) ways the piece raises readers' awareness, and (d) ways the writer brings the commentary to life.

2. Review "Research Update" (285) with students. Discuss I-Search principles and show them how journal entries can be prewriting for a personal commentary.

3. Have students think through the tension between the writer's perspective and the readers' by brainstorming two lists: My Perspective on the Issue, Popular Opinion on the Issue.

Related Workshops:

● Creating Connections, p. 89
● Improving Focus, p. 100

Write for College **References**

018 Selecting a Subject
021 Shaping a Subject
050 Writing with a Plan in Mind
110 Mastering the College Essay
244 Thinking Through an Argument
285 Research Update

Writing an Essay of Argumentation (232-237)

DISCUSSION: Students need to understand that the argumentation essay isn't a verbal fistfight. Rather, it explores and takes a reasonable stand on a debatable issue. Students should avoid writing papers that seek to promote either unexamined, set-in-concrete opinions or ambivalent positions of "It's all relative." Here are some keys to writing this type of essay:

1. **Writers may start with a strong opinion, but must be open to researching the topic until their position is fair and balanced.** Readers should not feel forced into accepting the argument.

2. **An effective argument has (a) a carefully worded claim; (b) reliable supporting evidence; and (c) logical reasoning about the evidence, both pro and con.**

Framing Questions:

- What debatable issues do I find intriguing or important for my life?

- What are the different sides of the issue? What claim do I want to make about the issue?

- How much do I know about the issue? What do I need to find out? Where can I find additional information?

- What are my reasons for making this claim? What evidence do I have to support my argument?

- What are the arguments against my claim? How should I concede or refute the counter-arguments?

- How should I organize my ideas? Should I make my strongest points first or last? When should I deal with opposing views?

Selecting Activities:

Warm-Up ● Have students discuss the following:

1. Topics they argue about with other students, coworkers, and family members

2. Hot topics such as divorce, immigration, sexual harassment, discrimination, private versus public schooling

Then discuss where arguments come from and how they get resolved.

Brainstorming ● (1) Write down "Now that's debatable!" and then explore the statement through listing or free writing. (2) Have students list communities they belong to and then explore issues, choices, and conflicts that divide each group.

In-Process Activities:

1. Assist students in stating their claims clearly.
   - Help students understand the different types of claims by giving them several controversial issues and asking them to draft claims of fact, value, and policy for each.
   - When students choose claims for their essay, have them define key terms and test their claims with their peers.

2. Use "Thinking Through an Argument" (244-246) to help students research and develop support for their claims and respond to each other's drafts.

3. Offer students the following traditional format for help with organizing their essays.
   - Introduce the topic and stress its importance.
   - Put the issue in context with background information.
   - Make your claim and develop a logical supporting argument.
   - Address counterarguments through concession and rebuttal.
   - Summarize main points and encourage readers to accept your claim.

Related Workshops:

- Achieving Economy, p. 94
- Evaluating Writing, p. 98

Writing a Position Paper

DISCUSSION: In a position paper, students explore an issue's "terrain" and locate a place to stand. Taking a stand allows them to compare positions, bravely defend their location, and get their bearings for future thinking, exploring, and acting. Here are some key instructions for your students:

1. **The goal is to develop a reasonable stand on an issue—and then to build a pathway to that position for your reader.** To convince readers to follow your path, adopt a positive, thoughtful tone—not a "love it or leave it" attitude.

2. **A strong position paper is rooted in personal commitment, not abstract theory.** Choose topics that affect one of your communities.

3. **Support your position by using persuasion's basics—claim, support, and reasoning—but also consider narrative.**

4. **Be willing to develop and modify your position through research.**

"Though old the thought and oft expressed, 'tis his at last who says it best."

—James Russell Lowell

Framing Questions:

◉ What issue is especially important for me? Why do I want to develop my position on it?

◉ What is my initial position on this issue? To what degree have I actually thought it through? What is the basis of my position—emotions, experiences, observations, upbringing, culture, ideas, readings?

◉ What research must I do in order to get my bearings, take a stand, and convince my readers?

◉ How has research modified my position?

◉ What strategies should I use to present my position and build a path to it for readers?

Selecting Activities:

Brainstorming ● Have students brainstorm important issues in the current political, social, economic, cultural, environmental, and educational realms. (Check out the "Essentials of Life Checklist" [019] for ideas or send students to newsmagazines.) Then have students rate each issue according to the strength of their feelings about it, the nature of their experience with it, and the depth of their knowledge about it.

Focused Assignment ● Focus the position paper on campus issues, career issues, or issues affecting the writer's generation.

In-Process Activities:

1. Help students think about their own position papers by having them review the handbook models:

   • What is your position on the essay's issue? In what ways is the issue debatable?

   • What stand does the essay take? Where is the stand stated?

   • Is the stand a "balanced" and reasonable one? How is it supported? How does the writer build a path between the reader and the position?

2. Encourage students to experiment with different placement for their position statements. What happens when they "state it" at the start? How does their paper change if they delay the position statement until the middle or the end?

3. Have students do peer reviews following these instructions:

   (a) Write your paper's topic at the top of the first page and then exchange papers.

   (b) Read your classmate's topic statement and draft a response to this prompt: "My first thoughts on this issue are . . . "

   (c) Read the paper and complete a second prompt: "Your paper affected my initial position on this issue by . . . "

Related Workshop:

● Improving Openings, pp. 91-92

Write for College References

017 A Guide to Prewriting
050 Writing with a Plan in Mind
060 Using Clear, Fair Language
110 Mastering the College Essay
244 Thinking Through an Argument
294 Writing Responsibly
536 Model Speech

Writing a Personal Response (249-255)

DISCUSSION: Good literature relates to readers' lives. Writing personal responses helps students explore that relationship as the writing process engages them in clarifying and developing their thoughts and feelings. Such responses enrich class discussion and motivate future writing. Here are some tips:

1. Students should understand the context of the response. What are the guidelines? What types of responses are expected—journal entries, creative poems, dialogues, essays? Will the responses be evaluated and used in class? (See pp. 12 and 16-22 in this manual for more on writing to learn.)

2. Good responses show meaningful interaction with a text. Focusing on what grabs their attention, students should explore impressions, questions, and connections with their experiences and other stories. Personal responses can take students within and beyond themselves.

3. Students should avoid responses that (a) simply say "I liked it" or "I hated it"; (b) focus only on the student's life or a summary of the plot; (c) try to say what the instructor wants to hear; (d) lack focus; or (e) preach.

4. A strong response begins with a "conversational" attitude. Students should approach any text with an open mind.

Framing Questions

⦿ Why do I want to respond to this work?

⦿ What thoughts and emotions are evoked by my first reading? Do I have a strong sense of what the author means and how the text works? What part of the work stands out for me? Why?

⦿ Upon rereading, what impressions, connections, and questions am I most interested in exploring?

⦿ What form should I use? How can this form expand, clarify, and deepen my thoughts and feelings about the text?

Selecting Activities:

Warm-Up ● Model a practice response in class. Give students a short poem or story to read. After they free-write a response, let them com-

pare responses. Afterward have them reflect on how their initial response may have changed.

Creative Options ● Give students choices. Let them select one poem from a set of poems, or one story from a group of stories. Encourage students to challenge themselves by responding to works that impress, excite, or puzzle them.

Focused Assignment ● Match the response assignment to the text and to the class. For example, students could write journal entries for a poetry or novel unit. Afterward they could write a response paper based on their journals. Be creative, flexible, and practical in your call for responses.

In-Process Activities:

1. Discuss the handbook models, keeping these questions in mind: (a) In what ways are these pieces "personal"? (b) What strategies does each writer use to focus her response?

2. Help students focus their responses.

• Direct them to "Four Ways to Talk About Literature" (201-202), "Starting Points for Journal Responses" (250), "Reading a Novel" (479), or "Reading a Poem" (480).

• Give them time to discuss their initial responses with peers in order to extend their thinking and feeling—to move from individual concerns to the larger literary conversation.

• Offer tips on note taking, annotating, journaling, and free writing.

Related Workshop:

● Finding a Form, p. 81

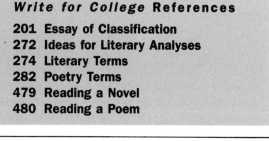

Writing a Review

DISCUSSION: In a review, writers create a conversation about literature by discussing a text's merits with their readers. Here are some tips for the review:

1. **An effective review evaluates a work using well-chosen criteria** (standards of judgment). The reviewer must know how literature works, and what makes it work well. For example, a writer judging a novel must understand character, plot, setting, point of view, style, and theme to effectively gauge the work.

2. **A review's readers generally haven't read the work but want help deciding whether or not they will.** A good review, then, makes careful reference to the work—giving enough information to help the reader form a judgment without giving away the story. Well-crafted summarizing and carefully selected quotations are key.

3. **The reviewer should avoid (a) judging without support, (b) providing an unbalanced evaluation, (c) using criteria that don't fit the work, or (d) simply presenting random thoughts on the work.**

"The literary work exists in the live circuit set up between reader and text: the reader infuses intellectual and emotional meaning into the pattern of verbal symbols, and those symbols channel his thoughts and feelings."

—Louise M. Rosenblatt

Framing Questions:

- What work (novel, poems, play, or concert) do I want to review? Why?
- What is my attitude toward this author, this genre of writing? Have I read this type of writing or this author's works before?
- What criteria for evaluation make sense for this work?
- What's my initial measure of the quality of this text?
- How does my personal experience affect my understanding and appreciation of the work?
- Who will read my review?
- How should I organize my review?

Selecting Activity:

Free Reading ● Make reviews part of students' independent reading. They can then share reviews that will assist their peers' decision making about future reading.

In-Process Activities:

1. Have students review the handbook models and bring in reviews from periodicals.
   - Discuss the information reviewers provide about the work through a summary or a quotation. What information has been held back?
   - Talk about the evaluation, the criteria used, and the support given.

2. Help students develop appropriate criteria. Go over the basics of the literary genre they are reviewing. Then let them free-write using this prompt: "A good novel (or short story, poem, play) should . . . "

3. Suggest students structure their reviews by trying the following:
   - Use the standard review format: (a) an introduction that puts the review in context and announces the writer's overall evaluation; (b) a summary of the work; (c) exploration of the work's strengths and weaknesses; (d) a conclusion that restates the judgment and advises the reader.
   - Answer questions that readers want answered: What's this work about? Will it hold my attention—entertain, inform, enthrall, challenge? Is it worth reading? How does it compare with other works from the same author or genre?

Related Workshop:

- Logical Organization, p. 88

Writing a Limited Literary Analysis (263-266)

DISCUSSION: While a personal response explores impressions and a review evaluates a text, a limited literary analysis interprets a text—without relying upon secondary sources. Here are some tips for effective interpretation:

1. **Interpretation begins with personal response.** An analysis should be a committed exploration of a work's meaning.

2. **Because readers will know the text already, analysis writers should aim to enrich understanding.** Extensive plot summary is not necessary.

3. **Interpretation involves an insightful, focused thesis about the work's meaning; a firm grasp of literary concepts; and a close reading that demonstrates a grasp of both the parts and the work as a whole.**

4. **A limited analysis can take various forms:**
   - Explication—line-by-line, stanza-by-stanza, or section-by-section exploration of a work—of a part or the whole
   - Analysis—tracing one issue throughout a text
   - Comparison/contrast—of two texts or of two elements within a text

"The world of the imagination is a world of unborn or embryonic beliefs."

—Northrop Frye

Framing Questions:

◉ What is my first response to the text—impressions, questions, feelings?

◉ What is the text's meaning as a whole?

◉ What specific part, issue, or concept would I like to explore in depth? Is that focus manageable for this essay?

◉ What approach do I want to take—explication, analysis, comparison/contrast?

◉ What connections and patterns could I look for during rereading?

◉ What insightful thesis can I offer? How can I support it?

Selecting Activities:

Clustering ● To help students match a text with an approach, have them (1) list texts they might write about, (2) select three, and (3) create a cluster of issues for each.

Review ● Have students review course readings, class notes, "Ideas for Literary Analyses" (272), and "Literary Terms" (274-283).

Focused Assignment ● Choose one poem, story, or play; one specific theme; or one specific form, such as the sonnet.

In-Process Activities:

In class, model the process of moving from the initial personal response to the final polished analysis. Select a poem or story to work through.

- Respond through free writing and note taking.
- Choose a focus by asking a pointed question or completing the sentence "This poem or story is one that . . . ."
- Reread, annotate, and take notes with the focus in mind.
- Review annotations and notes for patterns and connections.
- Write a working thesis statement.
- Outline support for the thesis.
- Draft an analysis with attention to opening, body, and closing strategies.

Related Workshop:

● Limiting Your Topic, p. 79

Writing an Extended Literary Analysis

DISCUSSION: In the extended literary analysis, a writer interprets a text based on his or her own reading of it, plus the observations of accomplished critics. Here are some tips:

1. **Extended analyses develop from critical approaches—reader-response, formalist, historical, or ideological.** (See 201-202.) Students' approach should "match" their text, grow out of their critical questions, be attentive to literary elements, and be focused enough to be manageable.

2. **Students must use source materials effectively.** Ideas, not sources, should dominate the essay. Secondary sources should extend the interpretation—not substitute for it—by clarifying background, lending authoritative support, or offering alternative readings. All references and quotations must be carefully integrated.

"The ability to interpret is not acquired . . . What is acquired are the ways of interpreting and those same ways can also be forgotten or supplanted, or complicated or dropped from favor."
—Stanley Fish

Framing Questions:

◉ What text do I want to explore in depth?

◉ What questions should I ask?

◉ What do secondary sources say about the text? Do they offer background, support, or alternative readings?

◉ How can I organize my analysis integrating primary and secondary references?

◉ Is my tone respectful of both the text and the reader?

◉ Does my title identify the author or text and imply my focus?

Selecting Activities:

Free Writing ● Encourage students to choose a text by free-writing about engaging works.

Critical Approaches ● Discuss "Four Ways to Talk About Literature" (201-202). Have students list questions for their texts from each critical approach and then select an approach.

Focused Assignment ● Select one text and have students write analyses representing different critical approaches. Have students share their work, noting how the various approaches complement and clash with one another.

In-Process Activities:

1. Have students refine thesis statements by allowing peers to test them for clarity and complexity. Students should also "quiz" their own thesis, listing questions embedded in it, developing a forecasting statement about how the thesis will be proved, and finally drafting a working title.

2. Help students deal with sources:
   • Review types of secondary sources— author/work introductions; critical editions; periodical articles; CD-ROM's, videos, films, and on-line resources.
   • Model the pattern for using source materials in an essay: (a) make an interpretative point; (b) prepare for the quotation; (c) cite the quotation; and (d) comment on the quotation's significance.

3. Review drafts, asking students to answer the following questions about each other's work: What is the thesis, and is it thoroughly dealt with from the title through the conclusion? Does the introduction incite interest, introduce the thesis, and forecast the essay's direction? Are primary and secondary sources used to develop the analysis? Does the conclusion do more than repeat the thesis?

Related Workshop:

● Devising a Writing Plan, p. 80

Writing Workshops

Overview of the Writing Workshops

All of the writing workshops are organized according to the following headings and subheadings. An answer key for workshops calling for specific answers begins on page 127.

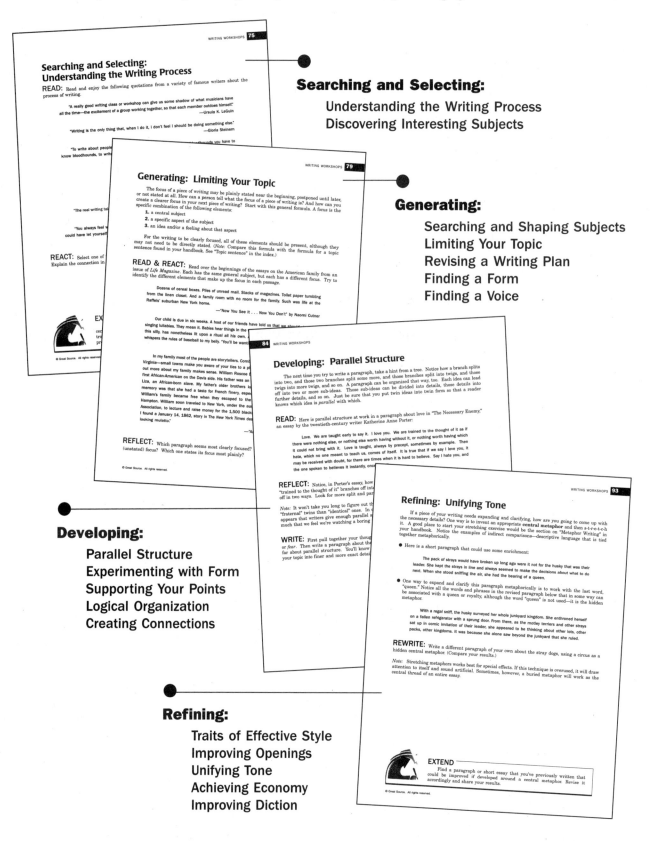

Searching and Selecting:
Understanding the Writing Process

READ: Read and enjoy the following quotations from a variety of famous writers about the process of writing.

"A really good writing class or workshop can give us some shadow of what musicians have all the time—the excitement of a group working together, so that each member outdoes himself."
—Ursula K. LeGuin

"Writing is the only thing that, when I do it, I don't feel I should be doing something else."
—Gloria Steinem

"To write about people you have to know people, ... as to write about bloodhounds you have to know bloodhounds, ..."

"The real writing tai...

"You always feel w... could have let yourself...

REACT: Select one of... Explain the connection in...

Searching and Selecting:

Understanding the Writing Process
Discovering Interesting Subjects

Generating: Limiting Your Topic

The focus of a piece of writing may be plainly stated near the beginning, postponed until later, or not stated at all. How can a person tell what the focus of a piece of writing is? And how can you create a clearer focus in your next piece of writing? Start with this general formula. A focus is the specific combination of the following elements:

1. a central subject
2. a specific aspect of the subject
3. an idea and/or a feeling about that aspect

For the writing to be clearly focused, all of these elements should be present, although they may not need to be directly stated. (*Note:* Compare this formula with the formula for a topic sentence found in your handbook. See "Topic sentence" in the index.)

READ & REACT: Read over the beginnings of the essays on the American family from an issue of *Life Magazine*. Each has the same general subject, but each has a different focus. Try to identify the different elements that make up the focus in each passage.

Dozens of cereal boxes. Piles of unread mail. Stacks of magazines. Toilet paper tumbling from the linen closet. And a family room with no room for the family. Such was life at the Raffels' suburban New York home.

—"Now You See It . . . Now You Don't" by Naomi Cutner

Our child is due in six weeks. A host of our friends have told us that we should singing lullabies. They mean it. Babies hear things in the... this silly, has nonetheless lit upon a ritual all his own. whispers the rules of baseball in my belly. "You'll be wanti...

In my family most of the people are storytellers. Comi... Virginia—small towns make you aware of your ties to a p... out more about my family makes sense. William Roscoe... first African-American on the Davis side. His father was an... Liza, an African-born slave. My father's older brothers k... memory was that she had a taste for French finery, espe... William's family became free when they escaped to the... Hampton. William soon traveled to New York, under the au... Association, to lecture and raise money for the 1,500 black... I found a January 14, 1862, story in *The New York Times* des... looking mulatto."

REFLECT: Which paragraph seems most clearly focused? (unstated) focus? Which one states its focus most plainly?

Generating:

Searching and Shaping Subjects
Limiting Your Topic
Revising a Writing Plan
Finding a Form
Finding a Voice

Developing: Parallel Structure

The next time you try to write a paragraph, take a hint from a tree. Notice how a branch splits into two, and those two branches split some more, and those branches split into twigs, and those twigs into more twigs, and so on. A paragraph can be organized that way, too. Each idea can lead off into two or more sub-ideas. Those sub-ideas can be divided into details, those details into further details, and so on. Just be sure that you put twin ideas into twin form so that a reader knows which idea is *parallel* with which.

READ: Here is parallel structure at work in a paragraph about love in "The Necessary Enemy," an essay by the twentieth-century writer Katherine Anne Porter:

Love. We are taught early to say it. I love you. We are trained to the thought of it as if there were nothing else, or nothing else worth having without it, or nothing worth having which it could not bring with it. Love is taught, always by precept, sometimes by example. Then hate, which no one meant to teach us, comes of itself. It is true that if we say I love you, it may be received with doubt, for there are times when it is hard to believe. Say I hate you, and the one spoken to believes it instantly, onc...

REFLECT: Notice, in Porter's essay, how... "trained to the thought of it" branches off int... off in two ways. Look for more split and par...

Note: It won't take you long to figure out th... "fraternal" twins than "identical" ones. In... appears that writers give enough parallel s... much that we feel we're watching a boring...

WRITE: First pull together your thou... or *fear*. Then write a paragraph about the... far about parallel structure. You'll know... your topic into finer and more exact detai...

Developing:

Parallel Structure
Experimenting with Form
Supporting Your Points
Logical Organization
Creating Connections

Refining: Unifying Tone

If a piece of your writing needs expanding and clarifying, how are you going to come up with the necessary details? One way is to invent an appropriate **central metaphor** and then s-t-r-e-t-c-h it. A good place to start your stretching exercise would be the section on "Metaphor Writing" in your handbook. Notice the examples of indirect comparisons—descriptive language that is tied together metaphorically.

● Here is a short paragraph that could use some enrichment:

The pack of strays would have broken up long ago were it not for the husky that was their leader. She kept the strays in line and always seemed to make the decisions about what to do next. When she stood sniffing the air, she had the bearing of a queen.

● One way to expand and clarify this paragraph metaphorically is to work with the last word, "queen." Notice all the words and phrases in the revised paragraph below that in some way can be associated with a queen or royalty, although the word "queen" is not used—it is the hidden metaphor.

With a regal sniff, the husky surveyed her whole junkyard kingdom. She enthroned herself on a fallen refrigerator with a sprung door. From there, as the motley terriers and other strays sat up in comic imitation of their leader, she appeared to be thinking about other lots, other packs, other kingdoms. It was because she alone saw beyond the junkyard that she ruled.

REWRITE: Write a different paragraph of your own about the stray dogs, using a circus as a hidden central metaphor. (Compare your results.)

Note: Stretching metaphors works best for special effects. If this technique is overused, it will draw attention to itself and sound artificial. Sometimes, however, a buried metaphor will work as the central thread of an entire essay.

EXTEND
Find a paragraph or short essay that you've previously written that could be improved if developed around a central metaphor. Revise it accordingly and share your results.

Refining:

Traits of Effective Style
Improving Openings
Unifying Tone
Achieving Economy
Improving Diction

Revising:
Advising in Peer Groups
Evaluating Style
Evaluating Writing
Adding Energy and Originality
Improving Focus
Crafting Sentences
Using Adverb Clauses

Editing:
Sentence Fragments
Complex Sentences
Relative Clauses
Parallel Structure
Consistency
Pronoun and Antecedent Agreement
Pronoun References
Dangling Modifiers
Sentence Errors
Economy

Proofreading:
Commas
Colons
Commas and Semicolons
Usage
Review
Caps, Numbers, and Abbreviations

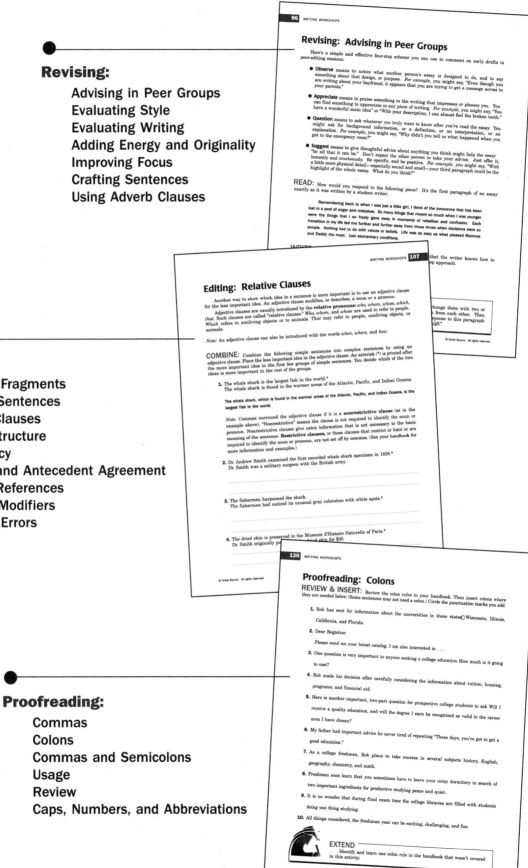

Implementing the Writing Workshops

The writing workshops can be implemented in a number of different ways to meet the students' needs. As noted below, they can work hand in hand with the forms of writing, serve as self-contained units for general instruction, or accommodate individuals who need enrichment work.

Integration into the Framework Writing Activities

Every effort should be made to integrate the writing workshops into the forms of writing framework activities. (Working on various writing skills and strategies always makes more sense in context during the composing process.) The "Instructor's Notes" for each framework activity cross-reference related writing workshops under "Related Workshops."

Classroom Instruction

Specific writing workshops can be used as the starting point or focus of instruction for the entire class. For example, instructors who feel the entire class could benefit from work on a particular skill–perhaps writing focus or thesis statements–could implement an appropriate workshop to meet this need.

Mini-Units

Instructors may decide to implement *mini-units* of related workshops (two-four days) for classroom instruction. If, for example, students need help with their revising skills and strategies, an instructor could implement two or three appropriate workshops (selecting from those listed under "Revising").

Small-Group Work

When members of a writing group share a particular concern (or need help with a particular problem) about their writing, instructors can direct them to an appropriate workshop for small-group work.

Individual Learning

The workshops can also be implemented on an individual basis (or in independent learning situations) to help specific students work on their basic writing skills.

Instructor/Student Conferences

When instructors and students meet one-on-one in a writing conference, instructors may use one of the workshops to illustrate a particular writing skill or strategy.

Searching and Selecting:
Understanding the Writing Process

READ: Read and enjoy the following quotations from a variety of famous writers about the process of writing.

"A really good writing class or workshop can give us some shadow of what musicians have all the time—the excitement of a group working together, so that each member outdoes himself."
—Ursula K. LeGuin

"Writing is the only thing that, when I do it, I don't feel I should be doing something else."
—Gloria Steinem

"To write about people you have to know people, to write about bloodhounds you have to know bloodhounds, to write about the Loch Ness monster you have to find out about it."
—James Thurber

". . . as soon as you connect with your true subject you will write."
—Joyce Carol Oates

"Easy writing makes hard reading."
—Ernest Hemingway

"The real writing takes place between the first miserable, crude draft and the finished thing."
—Gloria Naylor

"You always feel when you look it straight in the eye that you could have put more into it, could have let yourself go and dug harder."

—Emily Carr

REACT: Select one of the quotations that matches up well with your own writing experience. Explain the connection in a freely written exploratory draft. (Use your own paper.)

EXTEND

Write your own pithy statement about writing to be posted in a writing center. Review "Understanding the Process" in the handbook if you're having trouble coming up with ideas. (Refer to "Writing process, Understanding the process" in the index.)

Searching and Selecting: Discovering Interesting Subjects

"Writing is easy," said the well-known sportswriter Red Smith. "All you have to do is sit down at a typewriter and open a vein."

Right now, let's assume that you have been asked to "open a vein." Maybe your instructor has said, "You'll have 10 minutes for free writing." Free writing is also known as **impromptu writing**, **writing bursts**, or **stop 'n' write**.

Whatever the name, the problem is the same: how to get started, go hard, and bring your writing in for a landing without crashing and burning (i.e., getting writer's block). Nobody can give you strict rules for what is supposed to be a free and creative process. But you can learn to write better at high speed *if* you will learn how to talk to yourself as you write.

LISTEN: For this exercise you don't need to mumble or move your lips. Instead, activate the quiet voice inside your head that whispers encouragement to you as you're going along, a voice that improves your attitude, increases your energy, raises your ambition, and broadens your interest. Listen to some of the words a writer's brain might whisper:

get going

try it

faster, faster

use shorthand

what's it all about?

let go of yourself

what else?

what's the difference?

what comes next?

so what?

prove it

don't erase

show it

why?

how do I feel?

do some more

what do I think?

WRITE: Read these over and over until they start echoing in your brain. Now, start writing about a general topic of your own choosing. Let that little voice drive you on. *Never* talk back to it!

Note: The kind of free writing you'll be doing here is good for finding potential writing subjects as well as for shaping your initial thoughts about a subject already in hand. *However*, it is not as good for writing an essay answer on a test or turning in a quick diagnostic essay that shows your new instructor what an excellent writer you are. Formal impromptu writing calls for more discipline.

Generating: Searching and Shaping Subjects

READ: If you've already picked a topic, use the writing method called "cubing" to search your mind for more of what you already know. How many sides on a cube? That's easy: six. (Think of dice, whose sides are numbered for you.) You can use the six sides of a cube to remind you of six major ways to explore your topic. Suppose you've decided to write about the TV coverage of a major sporting event. Here is how you might "cube" your topic:

Side 1: Describe It

For 5 minutes, write at top speed about the sights and sounds (and maybe the tastes, smells, and physical feelings) that you connect with the TV broadcast. Describe it so that a reader feels he or she has been there.

> They put a camera right on the woman's skis while she was doing the slalom. I could hear the ripping sound of the edges of her skis through the ice crystals. The snow was spraying onto the camera lens and making circle rainbows . . .

Side 2: Compare It

For 5 minutes, write a comparison between the telecast you watched and something comparable to it: for example, a related personal experience or another channel's coverage of the same event.

> Because of the way the camera got down to the snow level and made you feel and hear every cut and hump and whoosh and stuff, I got more excited watching this broadcast than I did the one time I went skiing in person. When I went skiing, I couldn't hear much because I had a rotten earache from the wind, and I couldn't feel much because the boots and stuff were killing my feet. I was totally numb . . .

Side 3: Associate It

For 5 more minutes, write about something that in some odd way you connect in your mind with the telecast. Maybe it reminds you of an afternoon nap, or a carnival sideshow, or a really bad play.

> The telecast was like, let's see, okay, like a half-dream, when your mind is swirling with wild images part of the time but somebody keeps breaking in talking the rest of the time and spoiling the mood. These jerky announcers thought their jokes were worth more airtime than the skiing, but I wanted to stay caught up in the dream . . .

Side 4: Analyze It

For 5 more minutes, write about the different identifiable parts of the telecast.

> I could count about four or five parts to the broadcast. Or maybe not parts but layers. There was the obvious commercial layer, which kept breaking in about every seven or eight minutes. Then there was the chitchat layer, where the announcers talked about themselves, mostly . . .

Side 5: Apply It

For 5 more minutes, write about what the telecast is good for, what its results are, how it could be used, etc.

> Parts of this broadcast would work well for a ski school, since they showed some of the fine points about how a skier balances and absorbs shocks with the knees. Or a tape of the broadcast could be used in journalism school, to analyze the structure (and the faults!) of a typical sports broadcast . . .

Side 6: Argue for or Against It

For 5 more minutes, make a case pro or con—to keep the telecast or to dump it, to change it or to leave it the same. Argue for its style of presentation, or against its length, or whatever.

> I want to argue that sports broadcasters should change the ratio between their talk and the amount of footage they show of the actual sport in action. The ideal, from my perspective, would be about five minutes of action footage for every one minute of talk. And the talk should concentrate on what the athlete is doing and why, not on who went to what college, who's from what Swiss village, who's got a collection of beer coasters, and that kind of junk.

There. That's a little over one half-hour's work. By the time you're through, you'll know a lot more about what you already knew. You're practically guaranteed to come up with some new ideas in the process of cubing. You'll be surprised! Then you can take that new material and channel it into an improved draft of your writing.

WRITE: Select an appealing topic after reading the "Selecting a Subject" section in your handbook. (Refer to "Topics, Guidelines for selecting" in the index for this information.) First, free-write about this topic for about 5-8 minutes. Then search your mind for more ideas about your topic by cubing it. Or, if you have already written a poem, a story, an editorial, or an essay, cube that for new ideas. Underline any thoughts or phrases you especially like in your free writing and cubing.

Note: If you can't make a cube, toss a single die three or four times. Or, if you can't find a die, simply write about three or four of the instructions that interest you.

Generating: Limiting Your Topic

The focus of a piece of writing may be plainly stated near the beginning, postponed until later, or not stated at all. How can a person tell what the focus of a piece of writing is? And how can you create a clearer focus in your next piece of writing? Start with this general formula. A focus is the specific combination of the following elements:

1. a central subject

2. a specific aspect of the subject

3. an idea and/or a feeling about that aspect

For the writing to be clearly focused, all of these elements should be present, although they may not need to be directly stated. (*Note:* Compare this formula with the formula for a topic sentence found in your handbook. See "Topic sentence" in the index.)

READ & REACT: Read over the beginnings of the essays on the American family from an issue of *Life Magazine*. Each has the same general subject, but each has a different focus. Try to identify the different elements that make up the focus in each passage.

> Dozens of cereal boxes. Piles of unread mail. Stacks of magazines. Toilet paper tumbling from the linen closet. And a family room with no room for the family. Such was life at the Raffels' suburban New York home.
>
> —"Now You See It . . . Now You Don't" by Naomi Cutner

> Our child is due in six weeks. A host of our friends have told us that we should start now, singing lullabies. They mean it. Babies hear things in the womb, they say. My husband, who finds this silly, has nonetheless lit upon a ritual all his own. At night with a fairly straight face, he whispers the rules of baseball to my belly. "You'll be wanting to know about tagging up," he says.
>
> —"Family Talk" by Lisa Grunwald

> In my family most of the people are storytellers. Combine that with growing up in Hampton, Virginia—small towns make you aware of your ties to a place—and my romantic quest to find out more about my family makes sense. William Roscoe Davis, my great-grandfather, was the first African American on the Davis side. His father was an English sea captain and his mother, Liza, an African-born slave. My father's older brothers knew their great-grandmother; their memory was that she had a taste for French finery, especially things like perfume. In 1861 William's family became free when they escaped to the Union Army's Fort Monroe, near Hampton. William soon traveled to New York, under the auspices of the American Missionary Association, to lecture and raise money for the 1,500 blacks who were living around the fort. I found a January 14, 1862, story in The *New York Times* describing him as "a fine, intelligent-looking mulatto."
>
> —"American Album" by Thulani Davis

REFLECT: Which paragraph seems most clearly focused? Which one has the most implicit (unstated) focus? Which one states its focus most plainly?

Generating: Devising a Writing Plan

Mitchell Ivers, in *The Random House Guide to Good Writing*, identifies a six-step process that, if applied and practiced, will help turn uncertain writers into more confident and persuasive essayists. (Remember that the essay is the basic form of writing practiced in most school settings.)

REACT: Put Ivers' process into action by completing the following plan. Do your work on your own paper. (Share your work upon completion.)

1. Choose a subject about which you have a strong opinion. (Refer to "Topics" in the handbook index for ideas.)

2. Write a thesis statement, identifying what you would like to explain or prove about the subject. (Generally speaking, a dominant feeling or attitude about the subject is expressed in the thesis statement.)

3. Identify at least one important counterargument to your thesis. (That is, admit to a possible weakness in your way of thinking, or point out that there is another way to look at your subject.)

4. List five or six points in support of your thesis. (If you can't think of five or six, list as many as you can.)

5. Identify your most persuasive argument or point. (Put a star next to the strongest point you have listed in #4.)

6. Come to some conclusion about your argument. (Decide what it is you have proved or determined through your planning.)

WRITE: The next step is to put your plan into action by writing a first draft of your essay. Develop your writing freely, starting with your thesis statement and then incorporating other ideas from your plan. *A suggestion:* Deal with the counterargument early on, and save your most persuasive argument for the knockout punch near the end of your essay. (Continue working with your essay if you like how it is shaping up.)

Generating: Finding a Form

One way to generate a text is to make it somehow *imitate* your subject. How can your writing "imitate" your subject? Well, inspect the following paragraph about a demolition derby by essayist and novelist Tom Wolfe:

> The pack will be going into a curve when suddenly two cars, three cars, four cars tangle, spinning and splattering all over each other and the retaining walls, upside down, right side up, inside out and in pieces, with the seams bursting open and discs, rods, wires, and gasoline spewing out and yards of sheet metal shearing off like Reynolds Wrap and crumbling into the most baroque shapes, after which an ash-blue smoke starts seeping up from the ruins and a thrill begins to spread over the stands like Newburg sauce.
>
> —*Kandy Kolored Tangerine-Flake Streamline Baby*

Do you notice that the way the race happens is the way the sentence happens? The sentence is a "pileup," with words and phrases colliding everywhere. Does that give you some new ideas for developing your writing? Try letting the subject you are writing about suggest the writing's form. Make the form express your subject, even as your words show and tell about it.

IMITATE: For practice, write a paragraph describing a thunderstorm in a thunderstormy way. In other words, try to make your writing imitate your subject.

A Thunderstorm

Before you write, briefly consider the pattern of a thunderstorm: from calm to crescendo to climax to decrescendo to calm once again. Try to reflect that pattern in the shape and tone of your description:

....

....

....

....

....

EXTEND

Have somebody else react to your writing and offer some suggestions. Then put your new knowledge to work by writing an entirely different essay in which you take advantage of the possibilities of imitative form.

Generating: Finding a Voice

If you listen carefully to the words of a story, a poem, or an essay—especially if it is being read aloud—you will probably hear a voice that seems to speak from the text. This thing we call "voice" in writing is a result of several choices a writer has to make:

1. Who is doing the telling?

2. Is the teller speaking about something that *had* already happened, something that *has been* happening, something that simply *happened* in the past, or something that is *happening right now*? (In other words, is the overall verb tense in the past perfect, present perfect, simple past, or present tense? Refer to "Tense of verbs" in the handbook index for more information.)

3. Is the teller a participant in the action, an observer, or someone who somehow knows about it?

4. What is the teller's attitude toward the subject?

READ: Here is a paragraph from a college freshman's essay. Pay attention to the voice of the narrator. The writer is describing her kindergarten as if it were a job site.

> I can distinctly remember the first job I ever had: kindergarten student. The first lesson the students learned was entitled, "Handraising." Though the training was short, I soon understood that the tall lady was the foreman in charge. As one might imagine, we did not need to be reminded very often that we worked under her. After all, who dares to disobey a five-foot-six-inch giant in charge of hall passes and bathroom breaks?

REACT: How would you describe the voice of the narrator in this paragraph? Notice these things:

1. The student herself is doing the telling.

2. She uses the simple past tense. The present tense verbs she uses apply only to things that are continually the same, even in the present (for example, "who *dares* to disobey").

3. She was a participant and is now reflecting on the experience.

4. She sounds mock-serious and bemused.

REFLECT: Think about how you would tell this story using a different voice. Here are some options to choose from.

1. Who is talking? Try the teacher, another one of the kindergartners, the gerbil.

2. Verb tense: Try the simple present tense, the past perfect tense, or one of the other tenses.

3. Angle: Act as a participant in the action, an observer from a different angle, or someone who heard about the action from someone else.

4. Attitude: Try sounding horrified, amused, angry, relieved, or disgusted.

Write your choices here:

1. ....   **3.** ....

2. ....   **4.** ....

WRITE: Using the choices above as your guide, write a first draft of a story about your own grade-school experience.

Narrative voice should not be confused with the voice of a verb (see "Voice" in the index of your handbook). "Voice of a verb" refers to whether the verb in a sentence is active or passive—that is, whether the subject of the sentence performs or receives the action.

Developing: Parallel Structure

The next time you try to write a paragraph, take a hint from a tree. Notice how a branch splits into two, and those two branches split some more, and those branches split into twigs, and those twigs into more twigs, and so on. A paragraph can be organized that way, too. Each idea can lead off into two or more sub-ideas. Those sub-ideas can be divided into details, those details into further details, and so on. Just be sure that you put twin ideas into twin form so that a reader knows which idea is *parallel* with which.

READ: Here is parallel structure at work in a paragraph about love in "The Necessary Enemy," an essay by the twentieth-century writer Katherine Anne Porter:

> Love. We are taught early to say it. I love you. We are trained to the thought of it as if there were nothing else, or nothing else worth having without it, or nothing worth having which it could not bring with it. Love is taught, always by precept, sometimes by example. Then hate, which no one meant to teach us, comes of itself. It is true that if we say I love you, it may be received with doubt, for there are times when it is hard to believe. Say I hate you, and the one spoken to believes it instantly, once for all.

REFLECT: Notice, in Porter's essay, how emotions are divided into love and hate. Notice how "trained to the thought of it" branches off into three "as if's." Notice how "love is taught" branches off in two ways. Look for more split and parallel structures in the rest of the paragraph.

Note: It won't take you long to figure out that the "twins" in paragraphs like these are more like "fraternal" twins than "identical" ones. In other words, you won't find many perfect parallels. It appears that writers give enough parallel structure so that we can notice the parallel, but not so much that we feel we're watching a boring mechanical device like a teeter-totter or a pendulum.

WRITE: First pull together your thoughts on a different emotion, such as *anger, jealousy, joy,* or *fear.* Then write a paragraph about the nature of that emotion, using what you've gathered so far about parallel structure. You'll know your writing is going well if you find yourself working your topic into finer and more exact detail.

Developing: Experimenting with Form

After a caterpillar has slept for a while in its cocoon, it is transformed into a butterfly. Transformations occur in writing, too, when a writer takes the substance from one piece of writing and recasts it in a new form. You can use transformations to develop new drafts of your work, especially in the early stages of exploring. Read on to learn how these transformations work.

READ: Here are some short transformations to serve as illustrations. Start with a "base text" like this paragraph from a student's first draft:

> When I was little I had a great interest in drawing. Unfortunately, as I grew older, I neglected this talent, so I was very pleased when I came across piles of my artwork. By looking at these drawings, I was able to recall immediately what other interests I had when I was younger.

Transformation 1: List

Forgotten childhood interests—dinosaurs—airplanes—spaceships—horses—imaginary beasts

Transformation 2: Sentence Fragments

Came across my old artwork. Lots of drawings. In the attic. Took me back. Showed me myself. My interests. Crayoned rockets. Penciled dinosaurs. Poster-painted airplanes and fantastic beasts. Forgot about all that.

Transformation 3: Prepositional Phrases

In the attic. In a box. On paper. With crayon, poster paints, pencil, and construction paper. From the imagination. By me. After many years. Like a time machine.

Transformation 4: Poetry

I took the lid off my childhood
and there, in paint, pencil, and passion
were my long-lost dinosaurs,
the planes my dreams flew,
and the horses of many stripes.

REFLECT: Each one of these transformations brings out something new. The list brings out the contents of the pictures. The fragments sound like a mind thinking. The prepositional phrases lead to the concept of a time machine, and the poetry recaptures some of the feelings of childhood. Each offers a new slant on the topic.

WRITE: Choose a short piece of your own writing, something that you would like to develop further. Write as many different transformations of it as time and interest permit. In addition to the four types above, here are other transformations to consider. Make up others of your own.

- Describe only sounds.
- Write in exclamations!
- Turn it into questions.
- Write it as a play script.

Developing: Writing in Detail

If your writing just hangs there, lifeless, maybe that's because you're telling too much and showing too little. Lovely writing moves the way a hummingbird moves: it darts in to suck up the details and then backs up to look things over. If you spend all of your time looking things over, you and your reader will go hungry. (See "Details" in your handbook index for many examples of the way showing can give life to bland *telling* statements.)

READ: Here's a telling statement that may sound fairly interesting as it stands:

Roy's parents tended his knife wound in a way that showed how deeply they were suffering.

However, this sentence simply tells the reader what to think rather than leading a reader through the thought by showing details. Here is how the acclaimed African American writer James Baldwin *shows* the idea in *Go Tell It on the Mountain*: (To fully appreciate this paragraph, listen to it read out loud, and read it out loud yourself.)

His father and mother, a small basin of water between them, knelt by the sofa where Roy lay, and his father was washing the blood from Roy's forehead. It seemed that his mother, whose touch was so much more gentle, had been thrust aside by his father, who could not bear to have anyone else touch his wounded son. And now she watched, one hand in the water, the other in a kind of anguish, at her waist. . . . Her face, as she watched, was full of pain and fear, of tension basely supported, and of pity that could scarcely have been expressed had she filled all the world with her weeping. His father muttered sweet, delirious things to Roy, and his hands, when he dipped them again in the basin and wrung out the cloth, were trembling.

REFLECT: How do you "show" in writing? Think in terms of the 5W's and H (*Who? What? When? Where? Why?* and *How?*). Make sure that your writing answers these questions. Also think in terms of the three different types of details: sensory, memory, and reflective. Refer to "Details" in the index of your handbook.

WRITE: Here are three sentences that tell rather than show. Raise at least one of them from the dead in a "showing" paragraph full of detail. (If none of these sentences suit you, think up your own telling sentence.) Share your results.

1. I had never seen anything like it before.

2. It was a thoughtless thing to do.

3. We could tell my teacher (coach, friend, etc.) was getting mad.

Developing: Supporting Your Points

If you state an important idea in writing, your readers will know what you think. But if you back up your statement with solid facts and figures, your readers may also begin to believe that what you think is true. For that reason, experienced writers stay alert for quotations, anecdotes, details, and provable facts that they can use to support their ideas.

READ: Here are some quotations, anecdotes, details, and provable facts that a writer might store away in his or her memory, hoping someday to use them in writing:

Quotations:

1. "I shut my eyes in order to see." (French painter Paul Gauguin)

2. "Happiness is a butterfly, which when pursued is always just beyond your grasp, but which, if you will sit down quietly, may alight upon you." (Nathaniel Hawthorne)

Anecdotes:

1. When asked why he wanted to become president, John F. Kennedy replied, "Because that's where the power is!"

2. A certain professor was married to the Countess of Malta. They celebrated their honeymoon aboard the *Andrea Doria*, which had the great misfortune to sink midway through their celebration. He always kept a model of the ship on his desk. When asked why, he would reply, "To remind me that each day could be my last."

Provable Facts and Details:

1. South African black nationalist Nelson R. Mandela was released from prison in 1990, after spending almost 28 years behind bars.

2. Ten of the 13 books that sold more than a million copies during the 1980s were written by only three authors: political-thriller writer Tom Clancy, horror writer Stephen King, and romance novelist Danielle Steele.

REFLECT: In your writing, which should come first, your thoughts or the support you borrow from an authority? Use common sense: If your ideas spring from the words of an authority, place the borrowed material first and follow with your commentary. If you borrow material to support an idea of your own, place your idea first.

WRITE: Practice incorporating borrowed material into your writing. Write a short paragraph that uses one of the tidbits above to reinforce something you have to say.

INSIDE info

Generally, offering plenty of support for your ideas is desirable. However, if you supply too much support and not enough personal statement or commentary, your own voice may be drowned out. Remember that support must support *something*, and that something is your own line of thought.

Developing: Logical Organization

There are two distinct ways to arrange the details in your writing: *inductively* and *deductively*. Watch how two different kinds of paragraphs can be developed out of the same sentence. Here's the sentence that will serve as the main idea for each paragraph:

The winter of 1990-91 will be remembered as a costly one.

The first type of paragraph will be arranged inductively. In other words, the statements begin with specific details that eventually guide the reader toward the main idea.

Arctic air masses dipped repeatedly across the nation's midsection. The results were reported on the nightly news. In the Texas panhandle, pipes burst as cloudless skies brought a rare hard freeze. In Tennessee, some 200 cars piled up in a dense fog, and many lives were lost. Many were injured and one was killed in New York City as a short circuit caused by melting snow led to an underground train derailment. In California, old-timers couldn't remember a colder spell than the one that this year ruined nearly 85 percent of the citrus crop, most of the avocados, the strawberries, and the broccoli. The winter of 1990-91 will be remembered as a costly one.

The second type of paragraph is arranged deductively. In other words, the main idea comes first, followed by specific details that serve as illustrations, proofs, or explanations.

The winter of 1990-91 will be remembered as a costly one. As arctic air masses dipped repeatedly across the nation's midsection, the sad results were reported on the nightly news. In the Texas panhandle, pipes burst as cloudless skies brought a rare hard freeze. In Tennessee, some 200 cars piled up in a dense fog, and many lives were lost. Many were injured and one was killed in New York City as a short circuit caused by melting snow led to an underground train derailment. In California, old-timers couldn't remember a colder spell than the one that this year ruined nearly 85 percent of the citrus crop, most of the avocados, the strawberries, and the broccoli.

WRITE: Write a paragraph about some conflict at your school or in your city. Decide whether inductive or deductive organization is called for, and use that method consistently.

EXTEND

Find an article in a newspaper or magazine that is clearly inductive or deductive. Bring it in for a class discussion. Be able to point out the features of the article that make it an example of one or the other methods of organization.

Developing: Creating Connections

Transitional words between sentences and paragraphs reassure and steer readers along, giving writing a more pleasing flow. Let's see how a professional writer uses transitional words and phrases to link ideas . . . and smooth out the writing.

READ: Here is a passage from an article on allergies in the June 22, 1992, issue of *Time* magazine. The capitalized words create effective transitions between sentences and between paragraphs. You can learn about transitions simply by noticing them and thinking about how they work.

> Acute attacks of asthma occur when the bronchial tubes become partly blocked. FOR REASONS THAT ARE NOT ENTIRELY CLEAR, the lungs are overstimulated by viral infections, allergens or pollutants. The body RESPONDS by activating various defense cells from the immune system. THEIR MOBILIZATION causes the airways to swell. AT THE SAME TIME, the muscles surrounding the airways contract, cutting off airflow. WHEN THAT HAPPENS, asthmatics must inhale an adrenaline-like substance to stop the muscle spasm and reopen their airways.
>
> IF THE ATTACKS RECUR enough times, HOWEVER, the lungs do not return to normal. THEY CONTINUE to act as if they are being invaded by parasites. THIS constant STATE of inflammatory alert damages the bronchial walls, creating scar tissue. AS A RESULT, the airways can no longer clear the mucus that forms deep in the lungs. The ENSUING buildup reduces the flow of air and sets the stage for the next attack.

RESPOND: Write thoughtful answers to the following questions. Afterward, share your answers with a classmate.

1. Where do most of the transitional words appear in the sentences? Do you see a good reason for this pattern?

2. What makes the word "responds" a transitional word? What unwritten words after the word "responds" would refer to the previous sentence?

3. To what words in the previous sentence do the words "their mobilization" refer to?

4. From what you can observe about transitions in these two paragraphs, write two of your own personal "rules for transition."

Note: You'll find a complete list of transitions in your handbook. (Refer to "Transitions, Useful linking" in the index.)

EXTEND

Apply what you've learned about transitions in a two-paragraph passage in which you consider the effects that something new (3-D television, stricter college entrance requirements, etc.) would have on you and your peers. Explain to a classmate how you've used transitions in your writing.

Refining: Traits of Effective Style

Everyone has his or her own individual tastes. While I really like Mexican food (earthy and healthy), you might like Irish food (homey and hearty) or French food (bon appétit!). I like purple; however, you may go for chartreuse. I really dig the blues, but you may prefer heavy metal. With writing style, it's the same. Everyone has opinions about what makes for good writing.

REACT: What do you value in writing? What draws you to certain writers again and again? Is their writing fast paced, or highly descriptive, or a bit hard edged and sarcastic? And what do you strive for when you write? When are you most satisfied with your work? In the space provided below, list five things you like to see in writing (including your own). (You might, for example, enjoy writing that sounds friendly and unpretentious, like one person talking to another person.)

RECONSIDER: Review your list in light of what the handbook says about the traits of good writing. Turn to the handbook section "Traits of Effective Writing." (Refer to "Writing with style" in the index.) Review this section and note at least two things that you would add to your personal list of traits of effective writing. Share with a classmate the results of your personal inventory.

 Though there are certain traits of effective writing that are commonly recognized, each writer's style is different—that uniqueness is the ultimate element of an effective style!

Refining: Improving Openings

What can fishhooks teach you about writing? Consider the fishhook. Why does it work? It's got a curve to make it catch, a point to make it sink in, and a barb to make it stick. Oh yes, and there's the bait. Many writers speak of the need for a "hook" in their writing. The audience is the sea in which they fish. The reader is the fish they want to catch. The subject is the bait. The angle of approach is that curving hook. The surprise in the opening is the point that sinks in. And that little extra touch, that idea left open or that hint of things to come, is the barb that won't let the "hook" slip out.

READ: Here are the opening sentences or paragraphs from a number of published essays. As you read through these openings, see if you can catch on to the hook and barb in each one. (Share your thoughts.)

> According to the projections, crime was supposed to be under control by now. The postwar baby-boom generation, which moved into its crime-prone years during the early 1960s, has grown up, yielding its place to the (proportionately) less numerous baby-bust generation. With relatively fewer 18-year-olds around, we should all be walking safer streets.
>
> —James Q. Wilson and John J. Dilulio, Jr.,
> "Crackdown: Treating the Symptoms of the Drug Problem"

(*Hint:* What is the effect of the word "should" in the last sentence?)

> My, my, girls, what's all the fuss over the new "mommy test"? Hundreds of eager young female job seekers have written to me in the last few weeks alone, confident of being able to pass the drug test, the polygraph test, Exxon's new breathalyzer test—but panicked over the mommy test. Well, the first thing you have to grasp if you hope to enter the ranks of management is that corporations have a perfect right to separate the thieves from the decent folk, the straights from the druggies, and, of course, the women from the mommies.
>
> —Barbara Ehrenreich, "The Mommy Test"

(*Hint:* Can you tell that this opening is sticky with sarcasm?)

> In government circles it's called the "NIMBY problem." Whether the proposal is for AIDS clinics, halfway houses for prison parolees or dumps for toxic and nuclear waste, it is usually met by the opposition of citizens' groups who shout NIMBY—"not in my backyard!"
>
> —Ted Peters, "The Waste-Disposal Crisis"

(*Hint:* What is your emotional response immediately after you read the final phrase?)

The end of the world is coming—again: 989 years ago, as the odometer of Western history approached its first millennium, the whole of Europe was seized by a paroxysm of preapocalyptic shivers.

—Bill Lawren, "Apocalypse Now?"

(*Hint:* What is the tone of the word "again" in the first line?)

A very, very long time ago (about three or four years) I took a certain secure and righteous pleasure in saying the things that women are supposed to say.

—Gloria Steinem, "Sisterhood"

(*Hint:* Where do you suspect that the writer is leading? What makes you think so?)

REFLECT: How do you think the writers go from these openings to the next paragraphs? In many cases, there is some kind of turn—a *but*, or *yet*, or *nevertheless*, or *still*. (The writer does that when she or he knows the "hook" is set, and it's time to start reeling in the fish.)

WRITE: Here is a chance to practice writing "hooks" for three different kinds of essays: personal, subject (expository), and reflective.

1. **Personal** Write an opening sentence or two with a "hook" about an aspect of your life that you think might be fascinating to a reader.

2. **Subject** Write a "hook" opening to an essay in which you communicate some specialized knowledge you already possess.

3. **Reflective** Write a "hook" opening to an essay in which you propose how to correct the number one irritant in your life. (Be sure you have a proper audience in mind.)

Refining: Unifying Tone

If a piece of your writing needs expanding and clarifying, how are you going to come up with the necessary details? One way is to invent an appropriate **central metaphor** and then s-t-r-e-t-c-h it. A good place to start your stretching exercise would be the section on "Metaphor Writing" in your handbook. Notice the examples of indirect comparisons—descriptive language that is tied together metaphorically.

● Here is a short paragraph that could use some enrichment:

> The pack of strays would have broken up long ago were it not for the husky that was their leader. She kept the strays in line and always seemed to make the decisions about what to do next. When she stood sniffing the air, she had the bearing of a queen.

● One way to expand and clarify this paragraph metaphorically is to work with the last word, "queen." Notice all the words and phrases in the revised paragraph below that in some way can be associated with a queen or royalty, although the word "queen" is not used—it is the hidden metaphor.

> With a regal sniff, the husky surveyed her whole junkyard kingdom. She enthroned herself on a fallen refrigerator with a sprung door. From there, as the motley terriers and other strays sat up in comic imitation of their leader, she appeared to be thinking about other lots, other packs, other kingdoms. It was because she alone saw beyond the junkyard that she ruled.

REWRITE: Write a different paragraph of your own about the stray dogs, using a circus as a hidden central metaphor. (Compare your results.)

Note: Stretching metaphors works best for special effects. If this technique is overused, it will draw attention to itself and sound artificial. Sometimes, however, a buried metaphor will work as the central thread of an entire essay.

EXTEND

Find a paragraph or short essay that you've previously written that could be improved if developed around a central metaphor. Revise it accordingly and share your results.

Refining: Achieving Ecomony

READ: Most writers can leave out a great deal more in their writing than they think. For example, all of the words in parentheses in the following paragraph can be removed or simplified:

> At the game (that was played) last night between St. Thomas College and its archrival, Horton College, (the players who were considered the best on each team) (were injured) (in the course of the action). Marty Grunwald, (who plays for) St. Thomas, (received an injury to) her shoulder (when she collided) (without warning) with an opposing player (from Horton). (Regrettably,) (the force of the collision was responsible for) dislocating (her) right (shoulder). (Likewise, in a surprising coincidence), Cassie Ribero from Horton (also suffered a dislocated right shoulder) (in an accidental collision). (The loss of their top players was a disappointment to both teams). [103 words]

When all of the useless words are removed, the thought can be fully expressed in one smooth-reading sentence:

> At last night's college game between archrivals St. Thomas and Horton, Marty Grunwald and Cassie Ribero, team leaders for their respective schools, both dislocated their right shoulders in collisions with opposing players. [32 words]

REWRITE: With a partner, study the following paragraph adapted from an article in the November 1991 issue of *Scientific American*. Then cut or simplify all of the words and phrases that are unnecessary. Rewrite the paragraph on your own paper. Compare your results with other teams.

> Imagine in your mind, if you will, a pinball-type machine that actually propels tiny photons of light instead of the usual steel marble-like objects and that uses things like mirrors to function as bumpers. If you watch very carefully the path taken by a photon as it is fired with considerable force into play, it ricochets off the mirrors as if it were a solid object, like a rock. But if, as all this is going on, you stop observing with your eyes, things begin to get strange and unusual. Unlike a hard, metallic, round steel ball, the photon shatters into many wavelets, each wavelet taking a different route or path through the imaginary machine on which the game is being played.

Refining: Improving Diction

The **connotation** of a word is what it suggests or implies beyond its literal meaning. Careless writers sometimes lose sight of the connotations of their words and end up suggesting things they never intended. When you refine your writing, watch where your connotations are going. Better yet, take advantage of the possibilities for *coordinating* the connotations so that you subtly shape a reader's response.

READ & REACT: Fill in each blank below the paragraph with the word from the list that best fits the meaning and feelings being communicated. (*Note:* Several words will work in each sentence below; you must choose the word that best provides the sarcastically disapproving tone the writer wants.)

Too many times I have picked up the evening newspaper to see a photograph of a very ....1............ -looking person splashed all over the front page. Usually, this person has just gone through a ....2............ experience, like a car accident, a fire, or a shooting. You would think newspapers would use a little more ....3............ and not choose such pictures to ....4............ the front page of their papers. It's bad enough that these people have had to suffer a misfortune to begin with, and then to have their grief ....5............ for everyone to see all seems very wrong. It ....6............ their tragedy unnecessarily and makes it even more unlikely they will soon forget what has happened. They will be reminded over and over again by neighbors, friends, coworkers, and ....7............ just how "terrible" and "awful" and "frightening" all of this must have been. They will be forced to ....8............ an event weeks and months and perhaps years after it would otherwise have been forgotten. This is the power of the press—at its worst.

1. .... (unhappy, miserable, distressed, tortured)

2. .... (disagreeable, traumatic, bad, difficult)

3. .... (discretion, intelligence, sensitivity, compassion)

4. .... (brighten, appear on, emblazon, decorate)

5. .... (shown, reproduced, advertised, broadcast)

6. .... (inflates, builds up, supplements, exaggerates)

7. .... (pals, well-wishers, troubled people, acquaintances)

8. .... (relive, recall, remember, recollect)

Revising: Advising in Peer Groups

Here's a simple and effective four-step scheme you can use to comment on early drafts in peer-editing sessions:

- **Observe** means to notice what another person's essay is designed to do, and to say something about that design, or purpose. *For example*, you might say, "Even though you are writing about your boyfriend, it appears that you are trying to get a message across to your parents."

- **Appreciate** means to praise something in the writing that impresses or pleases you. You can find something to appreciate in any piece of writing. *For example*, you might say, "You have a wonderful main idea" or "With your description, I can almost feel the broken tooth."

- **Question** means to ask whatever you truly want to know after you've read the essay. You might ask for background information, or a definition, or an interpretation, or an explanation. *For example*, you might say, "Why didn't you tell us what happened when you got to the emergency room?"

- **Suggest** means to give thoughtful advice about anything you think might help the essay "be all that it can be." Don't expect the other person to take your advice. Just offer it, honestly and courteously. Be specific, and be positive. *For example*, you might say, "With a little more physical detail—especially sound and smell—your third paragraph could be the highlight of the whole essay. What do you think?"

READ: How would you respond to the following piece? It's the first paragraph of an essay exactly as it was written by a student writer:

> Remembering back to when I was just a little girl, I think of the innocence that has been lost in a pool of anger and mistakes. So many things that meant so much when I was younger were the things that I so freely gave away in moments of rebellion and confusion. Each transition in my life led me further and further away from those times when decisions were so simple. Nothing had to do with values or beliefs. Life was as easy as what pleased Momma and Daddy the most. Just elementary conditions.

WRITE: The above paragraph is not perfect. Don't assume that the writer knows how to improve it. Write tactful comments to the author using the four-step approach.

EXTEND

When you've made your own comments, exchange them with two or more others and compare your responses. Learn from each other. Then discuss with your partners what the very best response to this paragraph would be. By now, you should be "feeling your OAQS."

Revising: Evaluating Style

READ: Study the short essay of comparison below. Read it over once and react to it instinctively. How does the writing work for you? In what ways? Then read it again in light of what your handbook says about effective writing style.

My sister and I have absolutely opposite personalities. I'm methodical, cautious, organized. Jennifer's impulsive, scattered, and fun-loving. I live for the future. She lives in the moment. When we were kids, I used to exploit these differences in our personalities—using them as a weapon against her. Basically, I teased her to death. For instance, she has always loved food and used to scarf down anything sweet at the speed of light when she was little. Every time we went for a ride in my father's classic 1956 Riviera sedan, something we did most every Sunday, my parents would give us one treat apiece. Usually we'd get a candy bar, sometimes an ice-cream bar. She'd eat her treat in about 10 seconds. I'd peel the wrapper real slow-like, and then eat my treat in stages. The outside of the peanut butter cup first, of course, and then the peanut butter. I'd spend a quarter of an hour on the outside chocolate alone! And of course, she'd have to sit there, and watch me eat the treat she no longer had—hers was eaten, mine was a weapon of torture. One day when she had eaten her Rice Krispie treat, and I was eating mine one Krispie at a time, my parents cured me of my urge to tease. They made me give her half my treat! I'm still the most methodical person I know, but no longer when it comes to dessert.

REACT: How does this writing stack up against the traits or characteristics of an effective style? We've listed a number of common traits below. Write a brief response to each. Mention strengths as well as weaknesses in the style of the writing.

Design	**Freshness**
Concreteness	**Coherence**
Energy	**Correctness**

Remember: Your writing style comes from a series of writing choices you make. It is composed of your words, your sentences, and your paragraphs—nobody else's.

Revising: Evaluating Writing

Suppose a member of your writing group gave you a paragraph and asked you to review it. What would you say? What would you focus on? Here are some suggestions: When you review a piece of writing, start with a fair attitude, ready to notice both the good and the bad. Focus on the writing, not the writer. Be ready to pay close attention to everything about the writing, large features and small. And finally, organize your thinking by using a good set of criteria.

READ: Study the paragraph below. Then use the four statements below as a "measuring stick" for the quality of this paragraph. After you've read the criteria, reread the paragraph in light of them.

Driving Me Crazy

If there is one thing that really drives me crazy, it is getting stuck behind a car that is going way under the speed limit. And, naturally, this always seems to happen when I'm already well on my way to being late. A feeling of anxiety mixed with aggravation soon begins to surface in me as I wait impatiently for the solid yellow line to turn to dashes. When it does, I am frustrated further to find that cars are again coming from the other direction, and I must wait longer still. Finally comes the time when I'm free to pass. I switch on my blinker and start to accelerate into the other lane. But wait! The other car, which I am now alongside of, accelerates, not allowing me to pass. I look ahead to see that a car is now coming from the other direction, and I must slow down and get back into my lane. My aggravation turns to anger as the Sunday driver, still ahead of me, again slows down, and I'm right back where I started.

REACT: Here is a series of basic statements about a piece of writing. Indicate whether you mostly agree or mostly disagree with each statement you apply to "Driving Me Crazy." Afterward, write comments to explain each of your judgments.

Note: It's one thing to have good criteria, but you also have to set high standards for using the criteria. Think of a grocer with an expensive scale—she or he still has to keep the scale in good condition and read it accurately. When you apply the criteria to "Driving Me Crazy," consistently demand the most and the best from it. Avoid taking an all-accepting attitude.

1. The paragraph is fully developed.

2. The paragraph is well focused.

3. It has a clear and worthy purpose.

4. It is sure to please its intended audience.

HANDBOOK HELPER: In your handbook you can find a different set of criteria for evaluating a piece of writing. Refer to the list of "Traits of Effective Writing" (see the index under "Writing with style"). The traits include design, concreteness, energy, freshness, coherence, and correctness. Read this section and decide for yourself how our paragraph measures up according to these criteria. In which area is it strongest and in which is it weakest? What other traits does the most effective writing have?

Revising: Adding Energy and Originality

Have you ever finished a piece of writing, then read over your work, and finally, with profound critical insight, blurted out the word "blah"? Almost every writer feels that way sometime about his or her work. Some proceed to throw their work away. But that isn't necessary. Here are six questions you can ask yourself when you review. By reviewing, you can catch opportunities you missed the first time around:

1. Is your topic worn-out?

2. Is your purpose stale?

3. Is your voice unnatural or fake?

4. Is your organization predictable?

5. Is your focus unclear?

6. Do your sentences fall into a rut?

Notice, also, that these six are in descending order of importance. In other words, if your topic **(1)** is stale, don't worry yet about your organization **(4)** or your sentence structure **(6)**. If you change your topic, all of the next five aspects of your writing will change as well.

READ & REACT: Here's a challenge. Read the following paragraph, which most readers would probably consider boring, and examine each of the six aspects mentioned above until you've found the aspect that is most responsible for making it boring. Compare your reactions with someone else's. Then read the commentary below the paragraph. (No fair peeking!)

> **(1)** In today's society, there is much advertising to be found. **(2)** You can find interesting ads in magazines, and there are commercials on TV about every ten minutes or so. **(3)** A lot of people think the ads are better than the programs, and I kind of agree with them. **(4)** Maybe that's why there are so many ads, because people like them. **(5)** Someday maybe TV will be all ads and no programs. **(6)** Would you like that?

Working up from the bottom of the list, notice that the **sentences** are in a rut. Almost all have uninteresting subjects and verbs, and too many clauses start with "there is" or "there are." But the lack of **focus** is a bigger problem. Every sentence seems to have equal weight; therefore, none has special weight. The **organization** is an even bigger problem: it goes from a vast generalization to general observations about what "a lot of people" think to a half-hearted question addressed to some nameless "you." A bigger problem yet is the **voice**. It's tired, impersonal, and bored with its own subject. It has a short attention span. Worse yet, the writer's **purpose** is weak and indefinite. The writer seems simply to be trying to get through an assignment. Finally, and most boring of all, the writer's **topic** is too big, too ordinary, to be of any interest to a reader.

WRITE: Pretend the advertising paragraph was your own first draft. Now that you've reviewed it and seen its problems, write a thorough revision, any length, about some aspect of advertising. Make your revision better than the original in all six areas; but this time, start improving from the **top** of the list (your topic) and work your way down.

Revising: Improving Focus

Sometimes the meaning of an essay needs to be communicated in one crucial paragraph. That calls for a paragraph that has . . .

- a clearly stated main idea,
- details supporting that main idea, and
- an order that clarifies the relationship between the details and the main idea.

READ & REACT: One of the three passages below is a crucial paragraph from "The Black Writer and the Southern Experience," an essay by the celebrated novelist Alice Walker. The other two are imitations of the paragraph. Place the initials "AW" next to the paragraph you think Ms. Walker wrote. (Be prepared to discuss the reasons for your choice.)

Note: Look for the passage that is focused and clear, that contains a topic sentence and effective supporting detail. Also look for the passage that is worthy of someone of Ms. Walker's lofty stature as a writer.

1. Once, while in college, I told a Northern man that I hoped to be a poet. He suggested that just maybe a "farmer's daughter" might not be the right stuff for a poet. He had a point. But I wanted to write poetry that would be understood by my people, not by the Queen of England.

2. The richness of the black writer's experience in the South can be remarkable, though some people might not think so. Once, while in college, I told a white middle-aged Northerner that I hoped to be a poet. In the nicest possible language, which still made me as mad as I've ever been, he suggested that a "farmer's daughter" might not be the stuff of which poets are made. On one level, of course, he had a point. A shack with only a dozen or so books is an unlikely place to discover a young Keats. But it is narrow thinking, indeed, to believe that a Keats is the only kind of poet one would want to grow up to be. One wants to write poetry that is understood by one's people, not by the Queen of England. Of course, should she be able to profit by it too, so much the better, but since that is not likely, catering to her tastes would be a waste of time.

3. Once, while in college, I told a middle-aged Northerner that I hoped to be a poet. In polite but maddening language, he suggested that a "farmer's daughter" might not be poet material. Okay, so maybe he did have a point. A shack with only a few books is an unusual place to find a young Keats. But I didn't want to grow up to be another Keats. I wanted to write poetry for my own people, not for the Queen of England. If she could profit by it too, so much the better.

EXTEND

Locate the crucial paragraph in one of your own essays. Does it have a clearly stated main idea, sufficient supporting detail, and a sense of order? Discuss the paragraph with a classmate.

Revising: Crafting Sentences

When a sentence begins, readers want to know what it's about. Then they want to know where it's going. When they move to the next sentence, they want to know whether it's going to be about the same thing, or whether it will move on to something new. Sensitive writers try to give their readers clues about such things. As clues, they use *repeated subjects*, *pronouns*, *synonyms*, and *transitional words* or *phrases*.

If you want to help your readers follow your line of thinking, remember these points:

● Shove toward the LEFT—that is, toward the beginning of your sentence—key words that name your topic and any transitional words or phrases that link your sentence to the sentence before it.

● Shove toward the RIGHT—that is, toward the end of your sentence—any words or phrases you want to emphasize because they are new, surprising, or important.

● When you move to the subject of the next sentence, try to echo one of the key words in the previous sentence. (The most obvious word to echo is the SUBJECT of the previous sentence. That keeps you on course.)

Note how the subject is echoed in the following two sentences:

In my culture, **CARS** are very large and lethal toys.
THEY tempt speed demons like me to play in dangerous ways.

REACT: Find a magazine article or a piece of your own writing to analyze in terms of its direction and flow. (Focus your attention on two or three longer paragraphs.) Points to consider in your analysis:

● Does the writer echo a key word in a previous sentence when he or she moves on to a new thought? (*Underline examples.*)

● Does the writer use specific transitional words or phrases? (*Circle examples.*)

● What is the overall effectiveness or smoothness of the piece? Does it clearly and effectively move from one point to the next? (*Explain*)

● What else might the writer have done to enable the flow of ideas?

● Has the article reinforced or changed your feelings about the construction of writing?

EXTEND

Write freely and reflectively about an experience or a phase in your life (as a team member, as an employee, as a newcomer). Afterward, analyze the direction and flow of your writing. Does it seem to naturally follow the "familiar first, new next" formula? Does it contain specific transitional words or phrases? Are key words echoed from sentence to sentence? What might you do to improve upon this initial writing?

Revising: Using Adverb Clauses

When you're a little child, ideas typically come to your mind one at a time:

> I want that ice-cream cone.

When you grow older, ideas may come in groups of two or three or more. And, as you speak or write, your mind is capable of sorting them in order of importance and linking them, putting some into main clauses and others into subordinate (or lesser) clauses, like this:

> If you're through licking that ice-cream cone, I want the leftovers so that I can curb my
> hunger pangs.

This sentence has two adverb clauses (subordinate clauses) that modify the verb in the main clause ("I want the leftovers").

Adverb clauses can be identified by the special function they serve and the distinctive words that introduce them:

- Some show the "time" of an idea related to the main idea. Watch for introductory words (called subordinating conjunctions) such as *before, after, when, until, since,* and *while.*
- Some show reasons "why." Watch for *because* and *since.*
- Some show "purpose" or "result." Watch for *that, so that,* and *in order that.*
- Some show "conditions." Watch for *if, unless, although, as long as,* and *even though.*

READ: Here is a short paragraph without any adverb clauses in it:

> The Converse Chuck Taylor All Star basketball shoe is an American classic. The company
> launched a series of TV spots. The shoe is less an athletic shoe than a fashion accessory.

REACT: Now turn the following sentences into adverb clauses and find a way to combine them with the main clauses in the paragraph above. For each adverb clause, use a subordinating conjunction that shows the relationship mentioned in parentheses. On your own paper, rewrite the whole paragraph, using adverb clauses effectively.

- It is now one of the cheapest shoes available. (*condition*)
- The company celebrated its 75th anniversary. (*time*)
- The public would continue to make the shoe its popular choice. (*purpose*)
- It was once the standard footwear of all self-respecting hoopsters. (*condition*)

EXTEND

Reread this workshop and find the following in it: a definition of "adverb clause" and the identifiers of an adverb clause.

Editing: Sentence Fragments

From elementary school onward, students are taught to avoid writing sentence fragments. However, lots of published writing contains fragments. Some fragments are written on purpose. So, while editing a manuscript, how will you decide whether to keep or correct a fragment?

READ: Here is a paragraph with some accidental fragments (italicized words). Read it carefully. Then change each fragment into a complete, effective sentence. (Refer to "Fragment sentence" in the handbook index for help.)

Both pleasant and unpleasant situations can cause stress. *Any incident that places a demand on you to readjust or change.* The reaction of the physical body to stress is the same. *Whether the stressor is pleasant or unpleasant.* A person can be completely free of stress. *But only after he or she dies.*

READ & REACT: Determine the stylistic purpose of each of these deliberate fragments.

● Everyone in our family, including my youngest sister, speaks German. *Fluently.*

● Mrs. Stokes: Weezie, come get your lunch, girl.
   Weezie: *No time. Lots of homework.*

● *A place to rest in the middle of the lagoon. Drips from the oars. Egrets flapping their wings.*

EDIT: In this paragraph underline the deliberate fragments but *edit* (correct) the accidental ones.

Time for recreation to ease your mind. Physical exercise to relieve physical and mental tension. Having a job that you enjoy, that you feel well-equipped to perform, and that others appreciate. These are a few of the keys to managing stress. But notice that recreation, physical exercise, and work are stressors in themselves. Dr. Selye, a physician from Montreal, Canada, who has authored several books on stress. Says that the reaction of the body to stress is the same. Whether the stressor is pleasant or unpleasant. Generally speaking, stress makes life more interesting. A person free from stress only when he or she dies. However, a type of stress called "distress" is harmful. Potentially. Distress can be caused by a daily job. That you dislike immensely. If you can exchange a distressing job for a more satisfying one. Do it. If not, talk over the pressures of work. With someone you trust and respect. Try to accept what you cannot change. And remember to leave time. For exercise and rest.

EXTEND
In a short paragraph deliberately use a few fragments for special effect.

Editing: Clarity

Would you like an easy and effective strategy for fixing problems with wording? All you have to do is use the 3 C's of editing.

Editing Code:

CUT [brackets]
If you find a part that's unnecessary or wordy, put brackets around it. If you decide that section is really unneeded, cut it!

CLARIFY ‿‿‿
If you see something confusing, unclear, or incomplete in your writing, put a wavy line under that section. You should rethink it, reword it, explain it, or add detail to it.

CONDENSE (parentheses)
If you come across a section of your writing that is wordy or overexplained, put a set of parentheses around it. (Refer to "Wordiness," "Deadwood, in sentences," and "Flowery language" in the handbook index for help.)

READ & REACT: Here is a marked portion of a student's in-progress essay using the 3-C's editing code. Rewrite the essay following the coding used. *Hint:* Start by reading the entire paragraph first; then cross out those sections in brackets and consider how to improve the sections in parentheses.

My most memorable experience was the first time I drove my dad's car. I was 15 years old [at the time], and we had just gone up to Saxon, Wisconsin, for the summer. My dad had to go into town [for something], and he let me drive his (pride and joy). (As I was going along, I could see out the corner of my eye that he was trying to be cool, but I could tell that he was [getting] tense) [and uptight]. Every time I would come to a stop, I could see him unconsciously trying (to put the brakes on). As we (were coming into town), we passed Old Dan's Bar. Everything was going great. [What a trip!] Then I noticed that he had his hands on the dashboard to brace himself. As I was watching him, I suddenly drove into a fire hydrant and totaled the front of my father's brand-new Buick. (Dear old Dad almost had a canary). He was so mad at me that he couldn't (say a word). [He was speechless.] After that he decided to turn around and go back to camp. When we got there, he got a Coke from the cooler, and he didn't talk to me until the next day. [Needless to say] the rest of our trip was (a real bummer) for me.

EXTEND

Compare your revisions of the above paragraph with a classmate's. What do the two of you agree on? Where do you disagree? Also: Evaluate one of your own essays using the strategy you just learned.

Editing: Complex Sentences

READ: As you revise, you may want to combine some of your short, simple sentences into more mature, efficient sentences. To join two ideas that are not equal in importance, you may use a **complex sentence.** A complex sentence contains one independent clause and one (or more) dependent clauses. The complex sentence is used to show the relationship of one idea to another.

The complex sentence helps you tell the reader which of the two ideas expressed in the sentence is more important. The more important idea (main idea) is placed in the independent clause; the less important idea is placed in the dependent, or subordinate, clause. Since the purpose of all writing is to communicate ideas clearly, the complex sentence is especially valuable to the writer.

An adverb clause is one kind of subordinate clause. Loosely speaking, it modifies a verb or another modifier in the sentence. It is easier to use adverb clauses effectively when you understand what they do in a sentence and become familiar with the subordinating conjunctions used to introduce them.

- Some subordinating conjunctions are used to introduce adverb clauses of **time:**
  before   after   when   until   since   while
- Some subordinating conjunctions introduce adverb clauses telling the **reason why:**
  because   since
- Some subordinating conjunctions introduce adverb clauses telling the **purpose or result:**
  so   that   so that   in order that
- Some subordinating conjunctions introduce adverb clauses telling the **condition:**
  whereas   if   unless   though   although   as long as   while

COMBINE: Combine each set of simple sentences into a complex sentence by placing the less important idea in an adverb clause. An asterisk (*) is printed after the more important idea in the first few sets. In parentheses after each of your new complex sentences, explain what your adverb clause tells.

1. Eagles will usually kill animals lighter than themselves.
Some fast-moving species have been known to carry off much heavier prey.*

Although eagles will usually kill animals lighter than themselves, some fast-moving species have been known to carry off much heavier prey. (condition)

2. The writhing, talon-pierced carp weighed 13 pounds.
The sea eagle flew low and was almost pulled underwater by its prey.*

3. The young eagle is heavier than its parents by as much as one pound.*
It leaves the nest.

4. The hunters looked up toward the mountain crest.
They saw an American bald eagle descending with a mule deer fawn in its talons.*

....

....

5. The lurid and suspicious stories continued to be printed.
Worried mothers lived in fear of their babies being carried off by eagles.*

....

....

6. Arthur Bowland once persuaded a Verreaux's eagle to snatch a 20-pound pack while in
flight. He could test the bird's supposed tremendous strength.

....

....

7. Scientific tests for muscularity and power will not be a true guide for the species.
They are done with wild, not captive, eagles.

....

....

8. Eagles can kill prey four times their own size.
They ordinarily cannot carry a load much over their own body weight.

....

....

9. Eagles will usually kill animals half their own weight or less.
They can get away easily with their dinner.

....

....

Editing: Relative Clauses

Another way to show which idea in a sentence is more important is to use an adjective clause for the less important idea. An adjective clause modifies, or describes, a noun or a pronoun.

Adjective clauses are usually introduced by the **relative pronouns:** *who, whom, whose, which, that.* Such clauses are called "relative clauses." *Who, whom,* and *whose* are used to refer to people. *Which* refers to nonliving objects or to animals. *That* may refer to people, nonliving objects, or animals.

Note: An adjective clause can also be introduced with the words *when, where,* and *how.*

COMBINE: Combine the following simple sentences into complex sentences by using an adjective clause. Place the less important idea in the adjective clause. An asterisk (*) is printed after the more important idea in the first few groups of simple sentences. You decide which of the two ideas is more important in the rest of the groups.

1. The whale shark is the largest fish in the world.*
   The whale shark is found in the warmer areas of the Atlantic, Pacific, and Indian Oceans.

   The whale shark, which is found in the warmer areas of the Atlantic, Pacific, and Indian Oceans, is the largest fish in the world.

   Note: Commas surround the adjective clause if it is a **nonrestrictive clause** (as in the example above). "Nonrestrictive" means the clause is not required to identify the noun or pronoun. Nonrestrictive clauses give extra information that is not necessary to the basic meaning of the sentence. **Restrictive clauses,** or those clauses that restrict or limit or are required to identify the noun or pronoun, are not set off by commas. (See your handbook for more information and examples.)

2. Dr. Andrew Smith examined the first recorded whale shark specimen in 1828.*
   Dr. Smith was a military surgeon with the British army.

   ....

   ....

3. The fishermen harpooned the shark.
   The fishermen had noticed its unusual gray coloration with white spots.*

   ....

   ....

4. The dried skin is preserved in the Museum d'Histoire Naturelle of Paris.*
   Dr. Smith originally purchased the dried skin for $30.

   ....

   ....

5. In 1868 a young Irish naturalist studied the whale sharks in the Seychelle Islands.*
He had heard the natives speak of a monstrous fish called the "Chagrin."

....

....

6. He saw several specimens.
The specimens exceeded 50 feet in length.

....

....

7. Many men reported sharks measuring nearly 70 feet in length.
These men had always been considered trustworthy.

....

....

8. The largest fish ever held in captivity was a whale shark.
It was kept in a small bay rather than in an aquarium.

....

....

9. The only other exceptionally large fish is the basking shark.
It compares in size with the whale shark.

....

....

10. A fish frightened millions of viewers during the movie *Jaws*.
The fish was a replica of the carnivorous great white shark.

....

....

Editing: Parallel Structure

Parallel structure is the balanced or coordinated arrangement of sentence elements that are equal in importance; in other words, it is the arranging of similar ideas in a similar way. The use of parallel structure can add a sense of rhythm and emphasis to your writing style that makes it more appealing to your reader. (Refer to your handbook for more information on parallel structure.)

REVISE: To better understand parallel structure, look at the sentences below. Each sentence contains two ideas or items that are equal in importance, but are not expressed in equal or parallel form. Those sentence parts that are not parallel and should be are underlined. Substitute a parallel expression in the place of one of those that is underlined. Revise each sentence as necessary so that the new expression fits in well and adds a sense of balance and rhythm to the overall sentence.

1. Swimming is an excellent exercise for strengthening your heart and one that will increase your lung power.

Swimming is an excellent exercise for strengthening your heart and increasing your lung power.

2. Swim for 10 minutes, dividing the time between the breaststroke, the crawl, and doing the backstroke, and you will have had a good workout.

....

....

3. Swimming improves the mobility of major joints and is strengthening for the muscles.

....

....

4. There is a rather odd myth that swimming in freezing water is beneficial and you will enjoy it.

....

....

5. At best, plunging into cold water may give you a kick; at worst, you may have a heart attack.

....

....

6. Some people get less exercise at the pool than they intend; they <u>talk to friends</u>, <u>tread water</u>, and <u>are hanging onto the side while watching others</u>.

....

....

7. Faithful practice will result in <u>a smooth swimming style</u> and <u>your breathing pattern will be efficient</u>.

....

....

8. A <u>steady ten-minute swim</u> would probably comprise a good workout while <u>swimming furiously for three minutes</u> would not.

....

....

COMPLETE: Complete each of the following sentences by adding a word, phrase, or clause that is parallel to the underlined portion of the sentence. (Each addition must be sensible as well as parallel.)

1. Sitting in the middle of his new dormitory room were <u>a suitcase</u>, <u>a box of books</u>, and ....

....

2. He hopes to get a job on campus either <u>working in the library</u> or ....

....

3. This Saturday night <u>some of my friends want to go to the football game</u>, <u>some want to go out for pizza</u>, and ....

....

4. This time should really be spent <u>planning for the future</u>, not ....

....

5. We drove all morning <u>to get to the taco stand</u>, and we drove all afternoon ....

....

Editing: Consistency

READ & REACT: Study the guidelines for subject and verb agreement in your handbook. In the exercise below, underline the subject and circle the correct verb choice in the parentheses.

1. <u>Half</u> of the dorms on campus (is, (are)) coed dorms.

2. Most of the students (is, are) upperclassmen.

3. The faculty (present, presents) a freshman orientation to school every year.

4. Some of the students (is, are) commuting to school every day.

5. The campus news (include, includes), among other items, a list of activities for the week.

6. Personal computing is one of the new classes that (is, are) being offered for the first time this semester.

7. None of the freshmen (realize, realizes) where the student union is located.

8. All of the campus organizations (is, are) looking for new members among the incoming freshmen.

9. This is one of the books that (is, are) required for the freshman English course.

10. Mathematics (is, are) a requirement for almost any field of study.

11. The cause of the bad grade (was, were) poor study habits.

12. Of the tests that (is, are) used for evaluating college applicants, the ACT test is used most frequently.

13. Some of the students (request, requests) a specific instructor for each course they take.

14. Business is one of the majors that (is, are) becoming more popular.

15. The reason for the long lines on registration dayy (was, were) the inefficient methods the school used.

16. Some of the students attending college today (is, are) required to attend all classes.

17. Any of the students missing classes (is, are) required to report the reason for the absence.

18. Statistics (is, are) not as difficult as calculus for most people.

19. The room and time slot that (was, were) assigned to this class have been changed.

20. The increased enrollment for the class (was, were) the reason for these changes.

Editing: Pronoun and Antecedent Agreement

READ & REACT: Study the rules in your handbook concerning agreement of pronouns and antecedents. Then underline the correct pronoun in each of the following sentences. Circle the antecedent.

1. For the (job hunter) to get the best possible job, (he or she, they) needs to have three or four job offers from which to choose.

2. Everyone looking for a job should be aware of the different methods of searching available to (him or her, them).

3. Every job hunter owes it to (himself or herself, themselves) to become acquainted with all phases of the job-hunting process.

4. Both Ashley and her friend, Shelli, use newspaper ads for new job leads that (she, they) then follow up with a phone call and a letter.

5. Neither Ashley nor Shelli expects to find the perfect job on (her, their) first attempt.

6. Sometimes job hunters try to make (his or her, their) availability known by placing ads about themselves and (his or her, their) job skills in newspapers.

7. Most colleges have especially good placement services because (they, it) understand that finding a good job is the major reason (their, its) students came to college in the first place.

8. Some colleges offer (its, their) students a complete job placement service, including placement help years after the students have graduated.

9. Other college offices, however, think they have done (its, their) job when they place the student once after graduation.

10. The private employment agency charges (its, their) customer only when (he or she, they) get(s) a job.

11. When employers use an executive search firm, (he or she, they) want the firm to hire people presently employed by other companies.

12. Both the employer and the job hunter can send (his or her, their) listings to a clearinghouse.

13. The U.S. government offers all (its, their) citizens a free employment service.

14. Everyone feels nervous during (his or her, their) first job interview.

15. Neither the interviewer nor those being interviewed want (his or her, their) interview(s) to go poorly.

Editing: Pronoun References

A pronoun is like the jacket you leave on a seat at a concert to show that the seat is saved. The jacket is not the person; it stands in place of the person. In the same way, a pronoun is not a noun; it stands in place of a noun, which is referred to as its "antecedent."

A pronoun works well when both the writer and the reader can tell exactly which word is its antecedent. But read the following sentence and notice what is wrong with one of the pronouns and its antecedent:

As she edged her car toward the drive-up window, it made a strange rattling sound.
(Does "it" refer to the car or to the window?)

This is an example of **indefinite pronoun reference.** The pronoun could be referring to either of two words in the sentence. To correct sentences like this, it is usually best to replace the indefinite pronoun with a noun, depending upon the meaning you wish to convey. (Rephrasing the sentences is also acceptable.) Here are two ways to correct the sample sentence:

As she edged her car toward the drive-up window, the car made a strange rattling sound.

As she edged toward the drive-up window, her car made a strange rattling sound.

CHALLENGE: Each of the following sentences has an indefinite pronoun in it. Correct each sentence so its meaning is clear, using the lines provided.

1. The team moved the wrestling mat off the gym floor so that it could be cleaned.

....

....

....

2. When Tara entered her program into the computer, it went completely haywire.

....

....

....

3. Alina asked her mother if she could carry one of the boxes for her.

....

....

....

4. Frank let Carlos know that his microphone wasn't working.

....

....

....

5. Check your papers for silly writing errors so that your teacher can enjoy **reading them.**

....

....

....

6. Shortly after the old car had been given a final coat of paint, it began to run.

....

....

....

EXTEND

Write three sentences of your own that contain indefinite pronoun references. Exchange your work with a classmate, and correct each other's sentences.

Editing: Dangling Modifiers

READ: What is wrong with the following sentence?

> After finishing her routine on the parallel bars, the judge gave Juanita the winning score.

It sounds as if the judge herself finished the routine, instead of Juanita. Why? Because of a mistake in the way the sentence is worded.

● To correct the mistake, we could change the opening phrase:

> After Juanita finished her routine on the parallel bars, the judge gave her the winning score.

● We could also change the main clause:

> After finishing her routine on the parallel bars, Juanita was given the winning score by the judge.

When a modifying phrase at the opening of a sentence does not match the subject of the sentence, it is called a *dangling modifier*. Dangling modifiers are a serious writing problem because they destroy the logic of a writer's statement.

HANDBOOK HELPER: Look up "Modifiers, dangling" in the index to your handbook. Then look up "Verbal." There you will find a description of three types of verbals: participles, infinitives, and gerunds. These three types of verbals are often found in dangling modifiers. Learn to recognize them and to understand the implied subject of the verbal. That will make fixing, or editing, dangling modifiers easier.

DIRECTIONS: Correct the following sentences by rewording either the modifying opening phrase or the main clause. If the sentence is already correct, place a *C* on the line.

1. Using a computer to help diagnose engine problems, the car was expertly repaired by our mechanic.

  Using a computer to help diagnose engine problems, our mechanic expertly repaired the car.

  ....

2. While playing the piano, our dog began to howl at me.

  ....

  ....

3. After writing spontaneously for half an hour, our teacher said we should gather in small groups to discuss our drafts.

....

....

4. Scanning the horizon, we spotted a faint plume of smoke.

....

....

5. To seal the bargain, the grocer and the supplier shook hands.

....

....

6. Afraid to look, the bobcat made Thurgood tremble with fear.

....

....

7. After finishing the first three courses of our meal, the server brought out the dessert tray.

....

....

8. Whipping the willow's branches back and forth, we huddled at the screen door to watch the wind.

....

....

9. Found reading by the light of a flashlight at midnight, Mrs. Reyez gently scolded the children and put them to bed—again.

....

....

Note: Always check your writing for phrase modifiers that are incorrectly "hanging out." They will destroy the logic of your ideas and weaken the overall effect of your work.

Editing: Sentence Errors

REACT: Carefully review the following paragraph, correcting any sentence errors as you go along. (You will find examples of sentence fragments, comma splices, and run-on sentences in the paragraph.) Cross out incorrect punctuation marks and add punctuation and capital letters as needed. (Refer to "Sentence, Writing effectively" in the handbook index for help.)

1   As a small child, he had always eaten jelly doughnuts for breakfast. Now,

2   however, at a plump and rather easily winded 29. He has switched over to granola

3   and skim milk. Along with his new eating habits, his looks are also beginning to

4   change. He wears his hair a bit longer in back and thinner on top and his shoes are

5   those flip-flop kind. That are good for lower back pain. He thinks about this as he

6   sits gazing out at the backyard, which the neighbor kid with the nose ring mows

7   every Saturday for a sawbuck. He wonders if the kid knows that a sawbuck is a

8   slang term for ten dollars. Maybe his younger brother Kevin is right in his appraisal,

9   maybe he is old-fashioned and far, far out of step. They had just gone out with their

10   parents the night before, a monthly guilt-abating ritual. Kevin had walked into

11   the restaurant and had scanned his brother's clothes and posture, in addition, he

12   had even seemed to scan his brother's thoughts, with slow-mounting amusement,

13   Kevin had said, "You look so . . . granola." Trying to disguise his obvious

14   embarrassment, the older brother had grabbed his keys and had headed for the

15   Subaru in the parking lot.

EXTEND

As you probably know, professional writers occasionally break the rules in their work. A writer might, for example, purposely use a series of sentence fragments or express a long, rambling idea. Try breaking or stretching the rules yourself in one of your upcoming pieces of writing, but do so carefully and selectively, with a clear purpose and desired effect in mind.

Editing: Economy

REACT: Make the following sentences more concise by eliminating *deadwood*, *redundancy*, and other wordiness. For clear definitions of each of these terms, consult the index to your handbook. Place parentheses around any unnecessary words or phrases that you find.

1. The former tenant (who had lived in the apartment before we moved in) painted all the walls (with a coat of) pink (paint).

2. The length of the average basketball court is normally 90 feet long.

3. The main reason he didn't pass the test is because he didn't study carefully or look over his class notes.

4. There are six students who volunteered on their own to clean up after the homecoming dance is over.

5. The mountain climber was unable to descend down the mountain by himself and needed the help of another climber to assist him.

6. The fragile vase, which would surely break if mishandled, was shipped "Special Handling" so that it would be handled with care.

7. The canceled game has been rescheduled for 8:00 p.m. tomorrow evening.

8. A portable radio can be carried anywhere and is especially handy for jogging, biking, and other outdoor activities.

9. As a general rule, he usually spends about one hour of his time each day reading.

10. Needless to say, wordiness is a writing problem that should be eliminated from all writing, which goes without saying.

11. The complex financial problem, which was not easy to understand, had caused the team to move to another city where the money issue was not such a big problem as it had been before.

Note: Compare your answers with a partner's. See who was able to remove the most words without changing the basic sense of the sentences.

Proofreading: Commas

READ & INSERT: Read and study the handbook rules on using commas. Then insert commas where they are needed in the sentences below. Circle each comma you insert. Some sentences may not need commas.

1. Yesterday in health class, we learned the Heimlich maneuver, a method of clearing a choking person's blocked airway.

2. The Heimlich maneuver not artificial respiration is used to save a choking victim.

3. Unless you act to save him or her a victim of food choking will die of strangulation in four minutes.

4. When using the Heimlich maneuver you exert pressure that pushes the diaphragm up compresses the air in the lungs and expels the object blocking the airway.

5. A friend of mine who had apparently paid attention to her first-aid class saved the life of a choking victim.

6. The victim who had been eating steak was forever grateful that my friend had learned the Heimlich maneuver.

7. That is why it is important for everyone to know how to perform this maneuver or to get quick professional help.

8. Whenever you think a situation is life threatening don't hesitate to call an ambulance or the rescue squad.

9. After calling for emergency help be prepared to state your name the injured person's name the address or place where the injured person is located and a brief description of what happened.

10. This is necessary so that the emergency personnel know exactly what they have to do when they arrive.

11. Remember that your objective to help save a life can be better accomplished when you remain calm and follow suggested procedures.

EXTEND

Commas are used to separate a *vocative* from the rest of the sentence. Do you know what that means? If not, find out by referring to your handbook.

Proofreading: Colons

REVIEW & INSERT: Review the colon rules in your handbook. Then insert colons where they are needed below. (Some sentences may not need a colon.) Circle the punctuation marks you add.

1. Rob has sent for information about the universities in these states: Wisconsin, Illinois, California, and Florida.

2. Dear Registrar

Please send me your latest catalog. I am also interested in . . .

3. One question is very important to anyone seeking a college education How much is it going to cost?

4. Rob made his decision after carefully considering the information about tuition, housing, programs, and financial aid.

5. Here is another important, two-part question for prospective college students to ask Will I receive a quality education, and will the degree I earn be recognized as valid in the career area I have chosen?

6. My father had important advice he never tired of repeating "These days, you've got to get a good education."

7. As a college freshman, Rob plans to take courses in several subjects history, English, geography, chemistry, and math.

8. Freshmen soon learn that you sometimes have to leave your noisy dormitory in search of two important ingredients for productive studying peace and quiet.

9. It is no wonder that during final exam time the college libraries are filled with students doing one thing studying.

10. All things considered, the freshman year can be exciting, challenging, and fun.

EXTEND

Identify and learn one colon rule in the handbook that wasn't covered in this activity.

Proofreading: Commas and Semicolons

INSERT: Place commas and semicolons where they are needed in the paragraphs below. Circle punctuation marks you add. (Remember to refer to your handbook if you have any questions about the rules for using commas and semicolons.)

1   One of the most remarkable and brilliant scientists of our time is 50-year-old

2   Stephen Hawking—physics professor, author, and theorist. His studies concerning

3   the nature of the universe and black holes have advanced our understanding of space.

4   More importantly Dr. Hawking has done more than any other physicist in describing

5   and detailing his life's work in language understood by the average person. In short

6   he has brought the outer limits of the universe "down to earth."

7   These accomplishments alone merit our praise and respect that Dr. Hawking

8   has accomplished them despite disabling personal setbacks is almost

9   incomprehensible. In 1962 when he was only 20 years old Stephen Hawking learned

10 he had amyotrophic lateral sclerosis or ALS. ALS gradually destroys the nerves and

11 muscles needed for moving. Doctors told him that he would probably die before he

12 finished his doctoral degree however Stephen didn't let their prognosis stop him. With

13 the support of fellow Cambridge student Jane Wilde whom he later married he

14 continued his studies and received his Ph.D.

15 During the course of his doctoral work Dr. Hawking became interested in the

16 work of scientist Roger Penrose an early theorist in the study of black holes. Black

17 holes are spaces that Penrose and Hawking believe exist in space. These spaces

18 possibly formed when a star burns itself out and collapses are areas in which gravity

19 is extremely strong anything pulled into the black hole cannot get out. Even time

20 stops!

21   Stephen Hawking's work on black holes and the nature of the universe was

22   published in a book entitled *A Brief History of Time: From the Big Bang to Black*

23   *Holes*. The book was written for people who do not have a scientific background. It

24   is a remarkable book. What makes it even more remarkable is that it was written

25   by a man unable to move his arms and hands to write unable to speak and unable

26   to communicate normally. The book is a testament to one person's determination to

27   succeed to be heard and to overcome personal tragedy.

EXTEND

One semicolon rule in your handbook states, "A semicolon is used to separate groups of words that already contain commas." Provide an example sentence illustrating this rule without looking in your handbook until after your sentence is written. Then refer to the handbook to check your work.

Proofreading: Usage

SELECT: As you carefully read through the following sentences, underline the correct word in each set of parentheses. (Refer to "Usage, mixed pairs" in the handbook index for help.)

1. Elisha attended the (<u>annual</u>, perennial) career fair at the local college.

2. She and her classmates had to (accept, except) (their, there, they're) invitations four weeks in advance in order to attend the fair.

3. (Already, All ready) the (amount, number) of people attending was (all together, altogether) too many.

4. Even though the (sight, site) of the fair was a large auditorium, (their, there) was hardly room for all those who came.

5. Elisha found she had no (personal, personnel) interest in the main speaker's topic, "Let astrology be (your, you're) career guide."

6. (Among, Between) the speakers at the fair were some very eminent members of the business community.

7. Still, (there, their, they're) were (fewer, less) speakers (than, then) Elisha anticipated.

8. At one point, Elisha had to (chose, choose) (between, among) visiting a college recruiter and a vocational counselor.

9. The vocational counselor presented her material (good, well) (accept, except) for those few times she was (to, too, two) (quiet, quite).

10. The booths of the college representatives were set up (beside, besides) the vocational representatives' booths.

11. (Further, Farther) down were the booths of the two-year and specialty schools.

12. The (continuous, continual) activity made Elisha very tired; still, she had to (compliment, complement) the organizers on a job well done.

Proofreading: Review

CORRECT: Proofread the essay below. Draw a line through any errors you find in capitalization, numbers, abbreviations, punctuation, spelling, and usage. Write the correction above each error. Add (and circle) punctuation as necessary. (*Hint:* Numbers are used frequently in this piece. Refer to the rules on "Numbers" in your handbook.)

1   About 450 miles off the coast of Newfoundland in 12,000 feet of water, scientists

2   have recently discovered the remains of the great ocean liner the S S Titanic. The

3   seventy-three year search for the Titanic, which went down in what is considered the

4   worlds' greatest sea disaster has been a challengeing one. It concluded finally in

5   September 1985. Because of this discovary interest in this legendary ship is stronger

6   then ever.

7   In part this interest may be due to the titanics reputation. When it was first

8   launched in 1912, the british steamer was the largest ship in the world. An incredible

9   882 ft. long and 175 ft. high, The Titanic was comparable to 4 city blocks in length

10   and 11 stories in hieght. It was proclaimed the most expensive most luxurious ship

11   ever built. It was said to be "unsinkable".

12   The later claim was the result of special features. The Titanic was equiped with

13   a double bottom and the hull was divided into 16 separate watertight compartments.

14   These added features, it was felt, would make the Titanic unsinkable.

15   Despite its reputation, the mighty Titanic did sink; and on its maiden voyage

16   too. Carrying approximatly 2200 passengers and over $420,000 worth of cargo, the

17   Titanic set sail from England in April, 1912, bound for New York. Just a few days

18   out of port, however on the night of April 14 the Titanic collided with an iceberg in

19   the north atlantic, ripping a 300 ft. gash along its starboard side. The mighty

20   "floating palace" sunk in a matter of 2 1/2 hours, taking with it all of its cargo and

21   1522 of its passengers.

Proofreading:
Caps, Numbers, and Abbreviations

IDENTIFY: Test your skill as a proofreader in the paragraphs below. Capitalize each letter that should be capitalized, punctuate or write out each abbreviation, use numerals or spelled-out numbers properly, and add or change punctuation as necessary.

1   Have you ever traveled to another country I know from personal experience

2   that living abroad can be an exciting and memorable adventure when I was twelve

3   years old my family spent 6 months in london england. we lived in a small Flat in

4   kensington gardens, kensington gardens is close to london the financial and fashion

5   center of england.

6   london is a fascinating city, it is filled with historical buildings such as the

7   houses of parliament the british museum and st pauls cathedral moreover it is home

8   to cultural sites such as the royal academy of arts. During our 6 month stay my

9   family spent countless hours walking through the british museum riding the double-

10   decker buses and retracing the steps of famous british poets and writers. it was in

11   london that I 1st discovered the differences between american english and the

12   queens english.

13   My introduction to the queens english was swift and confusing one day I started

14   out for the british museum but I got lost looking for the train. I stopped a

15   distinguished looking gentleman and asked him where I might find the train.

16   Train? he asked, looking confused.

17   yes, train. you know it goes underground . . . choo-choo, I replied.

18   He scratched his head, then said, train? Are you sure?

19   Yes, I replied. I know there's one nearby.

20   Suddenly he brightened. Ah, yes indeed, the tube.

21   Tube, I asked.

22   He smiled wisely. My dear young man in england its called the tube.

23   There were many other times I felt betrayed by my native language the british

24   say lift for elevator biscuits for cookies bumpershoot for umbrella. In short, theirs

25   is a very confusing english.

26   Although the language is confusing the weather often rainy and the food

27   different london is a magical city. The city itself dates back to the second century

28   and parts of londons early city can be seen in fragments of roman brick that are

29   visible in the walls of the tower of london. history buffs enjoy tracing the citys

30   development and growth during walking tours these tours take you through covent

31   garden the chief flower and fruit market fleet street the center of londons newspaper

32   industry and buckingham palace where one can still witness the changing of the

33   guard. London is a very special city and deserves a leisurely visit I'm glad I was

34   able to spend this time in another country. Its a time I'll never forget

EXTEND

Do you know which words in a title should be capitalized? Do you know the difference between an *acronym* and an *initialism*? And do you know how to express very large numbers in your writing? You'll find answers to these questions (and any other question you have about capitalization, abbreviations, and numbers) in your handbook. (Refer to "Checking Mechanics" in the Proofreader's Guide.)

Writing Workshops Answer Key

Answer keys are only supplied for workshops calling for specific answers. For the remaining workshops the answers may vary.

page 94 Refining: Achieving Economy

Instructor's Note: Here is the original paragraph as it appeared in *Scientific American*:

Imagine a pinball machine that propels photons of light instead of steel marbles and that uses mirrors as bumpers. If you watch the path of a photon as it is fired into play, it ricochets off the mirrors as if it were a solid object. But if you stop observing, things begin to get strange. Unlike a steel ball, the photon shatters into many wavelets, each taking a different route through the machine.

95 Refining: Improving Diction

1. tortured
2. traumatic or disagreeable
3. discretion or sensitivity
4. brighten or decorate or emblazon

5. broadcast or advertised
6. inflates or exaggerates
7. well-wishers
8. relive

100 Revising: Improving Focus

Ms. Walker wrote paragraph #2.

Editing: Sentence Fragments

From elementary school onward, students are taught to avoid writing sentence fragments. However, lots of published writing contains fragments. Some fragments are written on purpose. So, while editing a manuscript, how will you decide whether to keep or correct a fragment?

READ: Here is a paragraph with some accidental fragments (italicized words). Read it carefully. Then change each fragment into a complete, effective sentence. (Refer to "Fragment sentence" in the handbook index for help.)

Both pleasant and unpleasant situations can cause stress. *Any incident that places a demand on you to readjust or change.* The reaction of the physical body to stress is the same. *Whether the stressor is pleasant or unpleasant.* A person can be completely free of stress. *But only after he or she dies.*

READ & REACT: Determine the stylistic purpose of each of these deliberate fragments.

- Everyone in our family, including my youngest sister, speaks German. *Fluently.*
- Mrs. Stokes: Weezie, come get your lunch, girl.
  Weezie: *No time. Lots of homework.*
- *A place to rest in the middle of the lagoon. Drips from the oars. Egrets flapping their wings.*

EDIT: In this paragraph underline the deliberate fragments but *edit* (correct) the accidental ones.

Time for recreation to ease your mind. Physical exercise to relieve physical and mental tension. Having a job that you enjoy, that you feel well-equipped to perform, and that others appreciate. These are a few of the keys to managing stress. But notice that recreation, physical exercise, and work are stressors in themselves. Dr. Selye, a physician from Montreal, Canada, who has authored several books on stress, Says that the reaction of the body to stress is the same. Whether the stressor is pleasant or unpleasant. Generally speaking, stress makes life more interesting. A person free from stress only when he or she dies. However, a type of stress called "distress" is harmful. Potentially. Distress can be caused by a daily job that you dislike immensely. If you can exchange a distressing job for a more satisfying one, Do it. If not, talk over the pressures of work. With someone you trust and respect. Try to accept what you cannot change. And remember to leave time for exercise and rest.

EXTEND
In a short paragraph deliberately use a few fragments for special effect.

Editing: Complex Sentences

READ: As you revise, you may want to combine some of your short, simple sentences into more mature, efficient sentences. To join two ideas that are not equal in importance, you may use a **complex sentence**. A complex sentence contains one independent clause and one (or more) dependent clauses. The complex sentence is used to show the relationship of one idea to another.

The complex sentence helps you tell the reader which of the two ideas expressed in the sentence is more important. The more important idea (main idea) is placed in the independent clause; the less important idea is placed in the dependent, or subordinate, clause. Since the purpose of all writing is to communicate ideas clearly, the complex sentence is especially valuable to the writer.

An adverb clause is one kind of subordinate clause. Loosely speaking, it modifies a verb or another modifier in the sentence. It is easier to use adverb clauses effectively when you understand what they do in a sentence and become familiar with the subordinating conjunctions used to introduce them.

- Some subordinating conjunctions are used to introduce adverb clauses of **time**:
  before   after   when   until   since   while

- Some subordinating conjunctions introduce adverb clauses telling the **reason why:**
  because   since

- Some subordinating conjunctions introduce adverb clauses telling the **purpose or result:**
  so that   in order that

- Some subordinating conjunctions introduce adverb clauses telling the **condition:**
  whereas   if   unless   though   although   as long as   while

COMBINE: Combine each set of simple sentences into a complex sentence by placing the less important idea in an adverb clause. An asterisk (*) is printed after the more important idea in the first few sets. In parentheses after each of your new complex sentences, explain what your adverb clause tells.

1. Eagles will usually kill animals lighter than themselves.
Some fast-moving species have been known to carry off much heavier prey.*

    Although eagles will usually kill animals lighter than themselves, some fast-moving species have been known to carry off much heavier prey. (condition)

2. The writhing, talon-pierced carp weighed 13 pounds.
The sea eagle flew low and was almost pulled underwater by its prey.*

    The sea eagle flew low and was almost pulled underwater by its prey, because the writhing, talon-pierced carp weighed almost 13 pounds. (reason why)

3. The young eagle is heavier than its parents by as much as one pound.*
It leaves the nest.

    The young eagle is heavier than its parents by as much as one pound when it leaves the nest.
    (time)

---

4. The hunters looked up toward the mountain crest.
They saw an American bald eagle descending with a mule deer fawn in its talons.*

    While the hunters looked up toward the mountain crest, they saw an American bald eagle descending with a mule deer fawn in its talons. (time)

5. The lurid and suspicious stories continued to be printed.
Worried mothers lived in fear of their babies being carried off by eagles.*

    As long as the lurid and suspicious stories continued to be printed, worried mothers lived in fear of their babies being carried off by eagles. (condition)

6. Arthur Bowland once persuaded a Verreaux's eagle to snatch a 20-pound pack while in flight. He could test the bird's supposed tremendous strength.

    Arthur Bowland once persuaded a Verreaux's eagle to snatch a 20-pound pack while in flight so that he could test the bird's supposed tremendous strength. (purpose or result)

7. Scientific tests for muscularity and power will not be a true guide for the species.
They are done with wild, not captive, eagles.

    Scientific tests for muscularity and power will not be a true guide for the species unless they are done with wild, not captive, eagles. (condition)

8. Eagles can kill prey four times their own size.
They ordinarily cannot carry a load much over their own body weight.

    Although eagles can kill prey four times their own size, they ordinarily cannot carry a load much over their own body weight. (condition)

9. Eagles will usually kill animals half their own weight or less.
They can get away easily with their dinner.

    Eagles will usually kill animals half their own weight or less so that they can get away easily with their dinner. (purpose or result)

Editing: Relative Clauses

Another way to show which idea in a sentence is more important is to use an adjective clause for the less important idea. An adjective clause modifies, or describes, a noun or a pronoun.

Adjective clauses are usually introduced by the **relative pronouns:** *who, whom, whose, which, that.* Such clauses are called "relative clauses." *Who, whom,* and *whose* are used to refer to people. *Which* refers to nonliving objects or to animals. *That* may refer to people, nonliving objects, or animals.

Note: An adjective clause can also be introduced with the words *when, where,* and *how.*

COMBINE: Combine the following simple sentences into complex sentences by using an adjective clause. Place the less important idea in the adjective clause. An asterisk (*) is printed after the more important idea in the first few groups of simple sentences. You decide which of the two ideas is more important in the rest of the groups.

1. The whale shark is the largest fish in the world.*
The whale shark is found in the warmer areas of the Atlantic, Pacific, and Indian Oceans.

   The whale shark, which is found in the warmer areas of the Atlantic, Pacific, and Indian Oceans, is the largest fish in the world.

Note: Commas surround the adjective clause if it is a **nonrestrictive clause** (as in the example above). "Nonrestrictive" means the clause is not required to identify the noun or pronoun. Nonrestrictive clauses give extra information that is not necessary to the basic meaning of the sentence. **Restrictive clauses,** or those clauses that restrict or limit or are required to identify the noun or pronoun, are not set off by commas. (See your handbook for more information and examples.)

2. Dr. Andrew Smith examined the first recorded whale shark specimen in 1828.*
Dr. Smith was a military surgeon with the British army.

   Dr. Andrew Smith, who was a military surgeon with the British army, examined the first recorded whale shark specimen in 1828.

3. The fishermen harpooned the shark.
The fishermen had noticed its unusual gray coloration with white spots.*

   The fishermen who harpooned the shark had noticed its unusual gray coloration with white spots.

4. The dried skin is preserved in the Museum d'Histoire Naturelle of Paris.*
Dr. Smith originally purchased the dried skin for $30.

   The dried skin, which Dr. Smith originally purchased for $30, is preserved in the Museum d'Histoire Naturelle of Paris.

5. In 1868 a young Irish naturalist studied the whale sharks in the Seychelle Islands.*
He had heard the natives speak of a monstrous fish called the "Chagrin."

   In 1868 a young Irish naturalist studied the whale sharks in the Seychelle Islands, where he had heard the natives speak of a monstrous fish called the "Chagrin."

6. He saw several specimens.
The specimens exceeded 50 feet in length.

   He saw several specimens that exceeded 50 feet in length.

7. Many men reported sharks measuring nearly 70 feet in length.
These men had always been considered trustworthy.

   Many men who had always been considered trustworthy reported sharks measuring nearly 70 feet in length.

8. The largest fish ever held in captivity was a whale shark.
It was kept in a small bay rather than in an aquarium.

   The largest fish ever held in captivity was a whale shark, which was kept in a small bay rather than in an aquarium.

9. The only other exceptionally large fish is the basking shark.
It compares in size with the whale shark.

   The only other exceptionally large fish that compares in size with the whale shark is the basking shark.

10. A fish frightened millions of viewers during the movie *Jaws.*
The fish was a replica of the carnivorous great white shark.

   The fish that frightened millions of viewers during the movie Jaws *was a replica of the carnivorous great white shark.*

Editing: Parallel Structure

Parallel structure is the balanced or coordinated arrangement of sentence elements that are equal in importance; in other words, it is the arranging of similar ideas in a similar way. The use of parallel structure can add a sense of rhythm and emphasis to your writing style that makes it more appealing to your reader. (Refer to your handbook for more information on parallel structure.)

REVISE: To better understand parallel structure, look at the sentences below. Each sentence contains two ideas or items that are equal in importance, but are not expressed in equal or parallel form. Those sentence parts that are not parallel and should be are underlined. Substitute a parallel expression in the place of one of those that is underlined. Revise each sentence as necessary so that the new expression fits in well and adds a sense of balance and rhythm to the overall sentence.

1. Swimming is an excellent exercise for strengthening your heart and one that will increase your lung power.

   Swimming is an excellent exercise for strengthening your heart and increasing your lung power.

2. Swim for 10 minutes, dividing the time between the breaststroke, the crawl, and doing the backstroke, and you will have had a good workout.

   Swim for 10 minutes, dividing the time between the breaststroke, the crawl, and the backstroke, and you will have had a good workout.

3. Swimming improves the mobility of major joints and is strengthening for the muscles.

   Swimming improves the mobility of major joints and strengthens the muscles.

4. There is a rather odd myth that swimming in freezing water is beneficial and you will enjoy it.

   There is a rather odd myth that swimming in freezing water is beneficial and enjoyable.

5. At best, plunging into cold water may give you a kick; at worst, you may have a heart attack.

   At best, plunging into cold water may give you a kick; at worst, it may give you a heart attack.

---

6. Some people get less exercise at the pool than they intend; they talk to friends, tread water, and are hanging onto the side while watching others.

   . . . than they intend; they talk to friends, tread water, and hang onto the side while watching others.

7. Faithful practice will result in a smooth swimming style and your breathing pattern will be efficient.

   Faithful practice will result in a smooth swimming style and an efficient breathing pattern.

8. A steady ten-minute swim would probably comprise a good workout while swimming furiously for three minutes would not.

   . . . a good workout while a furious three-minute swim would not.

COMPLETE: Complete each of the following sentences by adding a word, phrase, or clause that is parallel to the underlined portion of the sentence. (Each addition must be sensible as well as parallel.)

1. Sitting in the middle of his new dormitory room were a suitcase, a box of books, and *a stereo.*

2. He hopes to get a job on campus either working in the library or *assisting in the lab.*

3. This Saturday night some of my friends want to go to the football game, some want to go out for pizza, and *some want to go to the movie.*

4. This time should really be spent planning for the future, not *thinking about the past.*

5. We drove all morning to get to the taco stand, and we drove all afternoon *to get back to our apartment.*

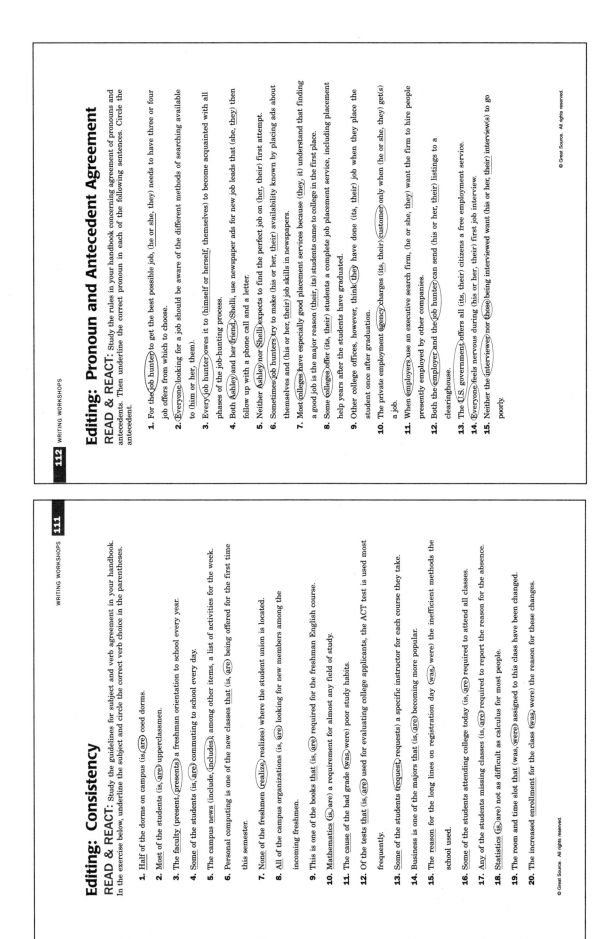

Editing: Pronoun and Antecedent Agreement

READ & REACT: Study the rules in your handbook concerning agreement of pronouns and antecedents. Then underline the correct pronoun in each of the following sentences. Circle the antecedent.

1. For the (job hunter) to get the best possible job, (he or she, they) needs to have three or four job offers from which to choose.

2. (Everyone) looking for a job should be aware of the different methods of searching available to (him or her, them).

3. Every (job hunter) owes it to (himself or herself, themselves) to become acquainted with all phases of the job-hunting process.

4. Both (Ashley) and her (friend) Shelli, use newspaper ads for new job leads that (she, they) then follow up with a phone call and a letter.

5. Neither (Ashley) nor (Shelli) expects to find the perfect job on (her, their) first attempt.

6. Sometimes (job hunters) try to make (his or her, their) availability known by placing ads about themselves and (his or her, their) job skills in newspapers.

7. Most (colleges) have especially good placement services because (they, it) understand that finding a good job is the major reason (their, its) students came to college in the first place.

8. Some (colleges) offer (its, their) students a complete job placement service, including placement help years after the students have graduated.

9. Other college offices, however, think (they) have done (its, their) job when they place the student once after graduation.

10. The private employment (agency) charges (its, their) (customer) only when (he or she, they) get(s) a job.

11. When (employers) use an executive search firm, (he or she, they) want the firm to hire people presently employed by other companies.

12. Both the (employer) and the (job hunter) can send (his or her, their) listings to a clearinghouse.

13. The U.S. government) offers all (its, their) citizens a free employment service.

14. (Everyone) feels nervous during (his or her, their) first job interview.

15. Neither the (interviewer) nor (those) being interviewed want (his or her, their) interview(s) to go poorly.

Editing: Consistency

READ & REACT: Study the guidelines for subject and verb agreement in your handbook. In the exercise below, underline the subject and circle the correct verb choice in the parentheses.

1. Half of the dorms on campus (is, are) coed dorms.

2. Most of the students (is, are) upperclassmen.

3. The faculty (present, presents) a freshman orientation to school every year.

4. Some of the students (is, are) commuting to school every day.

5. The campus news (include, includes) among other items, a list of activities for the week.

6. Personal computing is one of the new classes that (is, are) being offered for the first time this semester.

7. None of the freshmen (realize) realizes) where the student union is located.

8. All of the campus organizations (is, are) looking for new members among the incoming freshmen.

9. This is one of the books that (is, are) required for the freshman English course.

10. Mathematics (is, are) a requirement for almost any field of study.

11. The cause of the bad grade (was, were) poor study habits.

12. Of the tests that (is, are) used for evaluating college applicants, the ACT test is used most frequently.

13. Some of the students (request, requests) a specific instructor for each course they take.

14. Business is one of the majors that (is, are) becoming more popular.

15. The reason for the long lines on registration day (was, were) the inefficient methods the school used.

16. Some of the students attending college today (is, are) required to attend all classes.

17. Any of the students missing classes (is, are) required to report the reason for the absence.

18. Statistics (is, are) not as difficult as calculus for most people.

19. The room and time slot that (was, were) assigned to this class have been changed.

20. The increased enrollment for the class (was, were) the reason for these changes.

Editing: Pronoun References

A pronoun is like the jacket you leave on a seat at a concert to show that the seat is saved. The jacket is not the person; it stands in place of the person. In the same way, a pronoun is not a noun; it stands in place of a noun, which is referred to as its "antecedent."

A pronoun works well when both the writer and the reader can tell exactly which word is its antecedent. But read the following sentence and notice what is wrong with one of the pronouns and its antecedent:

As she edged her car toward the drive-up window, it made a strange rattling sound.
(Does "it" refer to the car or to the window?)

This is an example of **indefinite pronoun reference.** The pronoun could be referring to either of two words in the sentence. To correct sentences like this, it is usually best to replace the indefinite pronoun with a noun, depending upon the meaning you wish to convey. (Rephrasing the sentences is also acceptable.) Here are two ways to correct the sample sentence:

As she edged her car toward the drive-up window, the car made a strange rattling sound.

As she edged toward the drive-up window, her car made a strange rattling sound.

CHALLENGE: Each of the following sentences has an indefinite pronoun in it. Correct each sentence so its meaning is clear, using the lines provided.

1. The team moved the wrestling mat off the gym floor so that it could be cleaned.

   The team moved the wrestling mat off the gym floor so the floor could be cleaned.

   (OR) . . . so the mat could be cleaned.

2. When Tara entered her program into the computer, it went completely haywire.

   When Tara entered her program into the computer, the computer went completely haywire.

   (OR) . . . the program went completely haywire.

3. Alina asked her mother if she could carry one of the boxes for her.

   Alina asked if she could carry one of the boxes for her mother.

   (OR) Alina asked her mother to carry one of the boxes for her.

4. Frank let Carlos know that his microphone wasn't working.

   Frank let Carlos know that Carlos's microphone wasn't working.

   (OR) Frank's microphone wasn't working, so he let Carlos know.

5. Check your papers for silly writing errors so that your teacher can enjoy reading them.

   So that your teacher can enjoy reading all your papers, check them for careless writing errors.

6. Shortly after the old car had been given a final coat of paint, it began to run.

   The paint began to run shortly after the old car had been given a final coat.

EXTEND

Write three sentences of your own that contain indefinite pronoun references. Exchange your work with a classmate, and correct each other's sentences.

Editing: Dangling Modifiers

READ: What is wrong with the following sentence?

After finishing her routine on the parallel bars, the judge gave Juanita the winning score.

It sounds as if the judge herself finished the routine, instead of Juanita. Why? Because of a mistake in the way the sentence is worded.

● To correct the mistake, we could change the opening phrase:

After Juanita finished her routine on the parallel bars, the judge gave her the winning score.

● We could also change the main clause:

After finishing her routine on the parallel bars, Juanita was given the winning score by the judge.

When a modifying phrase at the opening of a sentence does not match the subject of the sentence, it is called a *dangling modifier*. Dangling modifiers are a serious writing problem because they destroy the logic of a writer's statement.

HANDBOOK HELPER: Look up "Modifiers, dangling" in the index to your handbook. Then look up "Verbal." There you will find a description of three types of verbals: participles, infinitives, and gerunds. These three types of verbals are often found in dangling modifiers. Learn to recognize them and to understand the implied subject of the verbal. That will make fixing, or editing, dangling modifiers easier.

DIRECTIONS: Correct the following sentences by rewording either the modifying opening phrase or the main clause. If the sentence is already correct, place a *C* on the line.

1. Using a computer to help diagnose engine problems, the car was expertly repaired by our mechanic.

   Using a computer to help diagnose engine problems, our mechanic expertly repaired the car.

2. While playing the piano, our dog began to howl at me.

   While I was playing the piano, our dog began to howl at me.

---

3. After writing spontaneously for half an hour, our teacher said we should gather in small groups to discuss our drafts.

   After we had written spontaneously for half an hour, our teacher said we should gather in a

   small group to discuss our drafts.

4. Scanning the horizon, we spotted a faint plume of smoke.

   C

5. To seal the bargain, the grocer and the supplier shook hands.

   C

6. Afraid to look, the bobcat made Thurgood tremble with fear.

   Afraid to look at the bobcat, Thurgood trembled with fear.

7. After finishing the first three courses of our meal, the server brought out the dessert tray.

   After we finished the first three courses of our meal, the server brought out the dessert

   tray.

8. Whipping the willow's branches back and forth, we huddled at the screen door to watch the wind.

   We huddled at the screen door to watch the wind whipping the willow's branches back and

   forth.

9. Found reading by the light of a flashlight at midnight, Mrs. Reyez gently scolded the children and put them to bed—again.

   When she found the children reading by the light of a flashlight at midnight, Mrs. Reyez

   gently scolded them and put them to bed—again.

Note: Always check your writing for phrase modifiers that are incorrectly "hanging out." They will destroy the logic of your ideas and weaken the overall effect of your work.

Editing: Economy

REACT: Make the following sentences more concise by eliminating *deadwood*, *redundancy*, and other wordiness. For clear definitions of each of these terms, consult the index to your handbook. Place parentheses around any unnecessary words or phrases that you find.

1. The former tenant (who had lived in the apartment before we moved in) painted all the walls (with a coat of) pink (paint).

2. The length of the average basketball court is (normally) 90 feet (long).

3. (The main reason) he didn't pass the test (is because) he didn't study carefully (or look over his class notes).

4. (There are) six students (who) volunteered (on their own) to clean up after the homecoming dance (is over).

5. The (mountain) climber was unable to descend (down) the mountain (by himself) and needed the help of another climber (to assist him).

6. The fragile vase(which would surely break if mishandled,) was shipped "Special Handling" (so that it would be handled with care).

7. The (canceled) game has been rescheduled for 8:00 p.m. tomorrow (evening).

8. A portable radio (can be carried anywhere and) is especially handy for jogging, biking, and other outdoor activities.

9. As a general rule, he (usually) spends about one hour (of his time) each day reading.

10. (Needless to say,) wordiness is a (writing) problem that should be eliminated from all writing(which goes without saying).

11. The complex financial problem(which was not easy to understand,) had caused the team to move to another city (where the money issue was not such a big problem as it had been before).

Note: Compare your answers with a partner's. See who was able to remove the most words without changing the basic sense of the sentences.

Editing: Sentence Errors

REACT: Carefully review the following paragraph, correcting any sentence errors as you go along. (You will find examples of sentence fragments, comma splices, and run-on sentences in the paragraph.) Cross out incorrect punctuation marks and add punctuation and capital letters as needed. (Refer to "Sentence, Writing effectively" in the handbook index for help.)

1   As a small child, he had always eaten jelly doughnuts for breakfast. Now,
2   however, at a plump and rather easily winded 29/ He has switched over to granola
3   and skim milk. Along with his new eating habits, his looks are also beginning to
4   change. He wears his hair a bit longer in back and thinner on top/ and his shoes are
5   those flip-flop kind/ That are good for lower back pain. He thinks about this as he
6   sits gazing out at the backyard, which the neighbor kid with the nose ring mows
7   every Saturday for a sawbuck. He wonders if the kid knows that a sawbuck is a
8   slang term for ten dollars. Maybe his younger brother Kevin is right in his appraisal/
9   maybe he is old-fashioned and far, far out of step. They had just gone out with their
10 parents the night before, a monthly guilt-abating ritual. Kevin had walked into
11 the restaurant and had scanned his brother's clothes and posture/ in addition, he
12 had even seemed to scan his brother's thoughts/ with slow-mounting amusement,
13 Kevin had said, "You look so . . . granola." Trying to disguise his obvious
14 embarrassment, the older brother had grabbed his keys and had headed for the
15 Subaru in the parking lot.

EXTEND

As you probably know, professional writers occasionally break the rules in their work. A writer might, for example, purposely use a series of sentence fragments or express a long, rambling idea. Try breaking or stretching the rules yourself in one of your upcoming pieces of writing, but do so carefully and selectively, with a clear purpose and desired effect in mind.

Proofreading: Colons

REVIEW & INSERT: Review the colon rules in your handbook. Then insert colons where they are needed below. (Some sentences may not need a colon.) Circle the punctuation marks you add.

1. Rob has sent for information about the universities in these states: Wisconsin, Illinois, California, and Florida.

2. Dear Registrar:

   Please send me your latest catalog. I am also interested in . . .

3. One question is very important to anyone seeking a college education: How much is it going to cost?

4. Rob made his decision after carefully considering the information about tuition, housing, programs, and financial aid.

5. Here is another important, two-part question for prospective college students to ask: Will I receive a quality education, and will the degree I earn be recognized as valid in the career area I have chosen?

6. My father had important advice he never tired of repeating: "These days, you've got to get a good education."

7. As a college freshman, Rob plans to take courses in several subjects: history, English, geography, chemistry, and math.

8. Freshmen soon learn that you sometimes have to leave your noisy dormitory in search of two important ingredients for productive studying: peace and quiet.

9. It is no wonder that during final exam time the college libraries are filled with students doing one thing: studying.

10. All things considered, the freshman year can be exciting, challenging, and fun.

EXTEND
Identify and learn one colon rule in the handbook that wasn't covered in this activity.

Proofreading: Commas

READ & INSERT: Read and study the handbook rules on using commas. Then insert commas where they are needed in the sentences below. Circle each comma you insert. Some sentences may not need commas.

1. Yesterday in health class, we learned the Heimlich maneuver, a method of clearing a choking person's blocked airway.

2. The Heimlich maneuver, not artificial respiration, is used to save a choking victim.

3. Unless you act to save him or her, a victim of food choking will die of strangulation in four minutes.

4. When using the Heimlich maneuver, you exert pressure that pushes the diaphragm up, compresses the air in the lungs, and expels the object blocking the airway.

5. A friend of mine, who had apparently paid attention to her first-aid class, saved the life of a choking victim.

6. The victim, who had been eating steak, was forever grateful that my friend had learned the Heimlich maneuver.

7. That is why it is important for everyone to know how to perform this maneuver or to get quick professional help.

8. Whenever you think a situation is life threatening, don't hesitate to call an ambulance or the rescue squad.

9. After calling for emergency help, be prepared to state your name, the injured person's name, the address or place where the injured person is located, and a brief description of what happened.

10. This is necessary so that the emergency personnel know exactly what they have to do when they arrive.

11. Remember that your objective, to help save a life, can be better accomplished when you remain calm and follow suggested procedures.

EXTEND
Commas are used to separate a *vocative* from the rest of the sentence. Do you know what that means? If not, find out by referring to your handbook.

Proofreading: Commas and Semicolons

INSERT: Place commas and semicolons where they are needed in the paragraphs below. Circle punctuation marks you add. (Remember to refer to your handbook if you have any questions about the rules for using commas and semicolons.)

1 One of the most remarkable and brilliant scientists of our time is 50-year-old

2 Stephen Hawking—physics professor, author, and theorist. His studies concerning

3 the nature of the universe and black holes have advanced our understanding of space.

4 More importantly, Dr. Hawking has done more than any other physicist in describing

5 and detailing his life's work in language understood by the average person. In short,

6 he has brought the outer limits of the universe "down to earth."

7 These accomplishments alone merit our praise and respect, that Dr. Hawking

8 has accomplished them despite disabling personal setbacks is almost

9 incomprehensible. In 1962, when he was only 20 years old, Stephen Hawking learned

10 he had amyotrophic lateral sclerosis, or ALS. ALS gradually destroys the nerves and

11 muscles needed for moving. Doctors told him that he would probably die before he

12 finished his doctoral degree, however, Stephen didn't let their prognosis stop him. With

13 the support of fellow Cambridge student Jane Wilde, whom he later married, he

14 continued his studies and received his Ph.D.

15 During the course of his doctoral work, Dr. Hawking became interested in the

16 work of scientist Roger Penrose, an early theorist in the study of black holes. Black

17 holes are spaces that Penrose and Hawking believe exist in space. These spaces,

18 possibly formed when a star burns itself out and collapses, are areas in which gravity

19 is extremely strong, anything pulled into the black hole cannot get out. Even time

20 stops!

21 Stephen Hawking's work on black holes and the nature of the universe was

22 published in a book entitled *A Brief History of Time: From the Big Bang to Black*

23 *Holes*. The book was written for people who do not have a scientific background. It

24 is a remarkable book. What makes it even more remarkable is that it was written

25 by a man unable to move his arms and hands to write, unable to speak, and unable

26 to communicate normally. The book is a testament to one person's determination to

27 succeed, to be heard, and to overcome personal tragedy.

EXTEND

One semicolon rule in your handbook states, "A semicolon is used to separate groups of words that already contain commas." Provide an example sentence illustrating this rule without looking in your handbook until after your sentence is written. Then refer to the handbook to check your work.

124 WRITING WORKSHOPS

Proofreading: Review

CORRECT: Proofread the essay below. Draw a line through any errors you find in capitalization, numbers, abbreviations, punctuation, spelling, and usage. Write the correction above each error. Add (and circle) punctuation as necessary. (*Hint:* Numbers are used frequently in this piece. Refer to the rules on "Numbers" in your handbook.)

1   About 450 miles off the coast of Newfoundland in 12,000 feet of water, scientists

2   have recently discovered the remains of the great ocean liner the S.S. Titanic. The

3   ~~seventy-three-year~~ search for the Titanic, which went down in what is considered the [73-year]

4   ~~worlds~~ greatest sea disaster, has been a ~~challenging~~ one. It concluded, finally, in [challenging] [discovery,]

5   September 1985. Because of this ~~discovery~~ interest in this legendary ship is stronger [Titanic's]

6   than ever.

7   In part, this interest may be due to the titanics reputation. When it was first

8   launched in 1912, the british steamer was the largest ship in the world. An incredible

9   882 ft. long and 175 ft. high, The Titanic was comparable to 4 city blocks in length [feet] [four]

10 and 11 stories in ~~hieght~~. It was proclaimed the most expensive, most luxurious ship [height]

11 ever built. It was said to be "unsinkable."

12 The ~~latter~~ claim was the result of special features. The Titanic was equipped with [equipped]

13 a double bottom, and the hull was divided into 16 separate, watertight compartments.

14 These added features, it was felt, would make the Titanic unsinkable.

15 Despite its reputation, the mighty Titanic did sink, and on its maiden voyage

16 too. Carrying ~~approximately~~ 2,200 passengers and over $420,000 worth of cargo, the [approximately]

17 Titanic set sail from England in April, 1912, bound for New York. Just a few days

18 out of port, however, on the night of April 14, the Titanic collided with an iceberg in

19 the north Atlantic, ripping a ~~300-ft.~~ gash along its starboard side. The mighty [300-foot]

20 "floating palace" sunk in a matter of 2 1/2 hours, taking with it all of its cargo and

21 1,522 of its passengers.

WRITING WORKSHOPS **123**

Proofreading: Usage

SELECT: As you carefully read through the following sentences, underline the correct word in each set of parentheses. (Refer to "Usage, mixed pairs" in the handbook index for help.)

1. Elisha attended the (annual, perennial) career fair at the local college.

2. She and her classmates had to (accept, except) (their, there, they're) invitations four weeks in advance in order to attend the fair.

3. (Already, All ready) the (amount, number) of people attending was (all together, altogether) too many.

4. Even though the (sight, site) of the fair was a large auditorium, (their, there) was hardly room for all those who came.

5. Elisha found she had no (personal, personnel) interest in the main speaker's topic, "Let astrology be (your, you're) career guide."

6. (Among, Between) the speakers at the fair were some very eminent members of the business community.

7. Still, (there, their, they're) were (fewer, less) speakers (than, then) Elisha anticipated.

8. At one point, Elisha had to (chose, choose) (between, among) visiting a college recruiter and a vocational counselor.

9. The vocational counselor presented her material (good, well) (accept, except) for those few times she was (to, too, two) (quiet, quite).

10. The booths of the college representatives were set up (beside, besides) the vocational representatives' booths.

11. (Further, Farther) down were the booths of the two-year and specialty schools.

12. The (continuous, continual) activity made Elisha very tired; still, she had to (compliment, complement) the organizers on a job well done.

Proofreading:
Caps, Numbers, and Abbreviations

IDENTIFY: Test your skill as a proofreader in the paragraphs below. Capitalize each letter that should be capitalized, punctuate or write out each abbreviation, use numerals or spelled-out numbers properly, and add or change punctuation as necessary.

1   Have you ever traveled to another country? I know from personal experience

2   that living abroad can be an exciting and memorable adventure. When I was twelve

3   years old, my family spent 6 months in london, england. We lived in a small flat in

4   Kensington gardens. Kensington gardens is close to london, the financial and fashion

5   center of england.

6   London is a fascinating city. It is filled with historical buildings such as the

7   Houses of parliament, the british museum, and st. paul's cathedral. Moreover, it is home

8   to cultural sites such as the royal academy of arts. During our 6 month stay, my

9   family spent countless hours walking through the british museum, riding the double-

10   decker buses, and retracing the steps of famous british poets and writers. At was in

11   london that I 1st discovered the differences between american english and the

12   queen's english.

13   My introduction to the queen's english was swift and confusing. One day I started

14   out for the british museum, but I got lost looking for the train. I stopped a

15   distinguished looking gentleman and asked him where I might find the train.

16   "Train?" he asked, looking confused.

17   "Yes, train. You know, it goes underground . . . choo-choo," I replied.

18   He scratched his head, then said, "Train? Are you sure?"

19   "Yes," I replied. "I know there's one nearby."

20   Suddenly, he brightened. "Ah, yes indeed, the tube."

21   "Tube?" I asked.

22   He smiled wisely. "My dear young man, in england it's called the tube."

23   There were many other times I felt betrayed by my native language, the british

24   say lift for elevator, biscuits for cookies, bumpershoot for umbrella. In short, theirs

25   is a very confusing english.

26   Although the language is confusing, the weather often often rainy, and the food

27   different, london is a magical city. The city itself dates back to the second century,

28   and parts of london's early city can be seen in fragments of roman brick that are

29   visible in the walls of the tower of london. History buffs enjoy tracing the city's

30   development and growth during walking tours. These tours take you through covent

31   garden, the chief flower and fruit market, fleet street, the center of london's newspaper

32   industry, and buckingham palace, where one can still witness the changing of the

33   guard. London is a very special city and deserves a leisurely visit. I'm glad I was

34   able to spend this time in another country. It's a time I'll never forget.

EXTEND

Do you know which words in a title should be capitalized? Do you know the difference between an *acronym* and an *initialism*? And do you know how to express very large numbers in your writing? You'll find answers to these questions (and any other question you have about capitalization, abbreviations, and numbers) in your handbook. (Refer to "Checking Mechanics" in the Proofreader's Guide.)

Daily Writing and Language Practice

Proofreader's Marks

Use the following proofreader's marks for correcting each MUG Shot sentence and paragraph.

Insert an exclamation point, a word, or a question mark.	∧	them ! Take∧home∧
Insert a colon, a comma, or a semicolon.	∧/ ∧/	Troy∧Michigan
Add a period.	⊙	Mrs⊙
Insert a hyphen or a dash.	⩗ ▽	one⩗third
Capitalize a letter.	/ or (≡)	T̸oronto (or toronto̲̲)
Make a capital letter lowercase.	/	h̸History
Close up space.	‿	ball‿park
Transpose.	∿	beleive
Replace or delete a word or phrase.	—— or ⟿	cold cold a ~~hot~~ day (or a ~~hot~~ day)
Add an apostrophe or quotation marks.	⩔ ⩖	Bill⩔s
Add italics.	——	Invisible Man
Add parentheses.	⩔ ⩔	letters⩔from A to Z⩔

Implementing the MUG Shot Activities

MUG Shot sentences and paragraphs contain errors in Mechanics, Usage, or Grammar, and are designed to develop students' editing and proofreading skills. Each sentence can be discussed and corrected during the first two or three minutes of a class, and the paragraphs can be used at the end of a week to review the week's sentences.

Planning

1. On the following pages, you will find seven sets of MUG Shot sentences and corresponding MUG Shot paragraphs. Each set consists of five sentences that contain a specific type of error. For example, sentences in the first set contain punctuation errors, and the corresponding paragraph contains similar types of errors.

2. If you want to focus on specific problems, select those sentences and paragraphs that contain the errors you want to discuss.

Introducing the Activity

3. On the days that you use the MUG Shot sentences, we suggest that you make an overhead projection of two or three sentences, project them on a screen at the beginning of class, and have students work together to correct the errors. Once you have completed a set of sentences, follow up with a paragraph that contains the same types of errors.

4. You may choose to make an overhead of the paragraph and project it on a screen, or you may decide to make copies of the paragraph and distribute them.

Evaluating the Students' Work

5. If you assign sentences often, we suggest that you evaluate the students' work at regular intervals (possibly every three weeks), and give a performance score. Three evaluative methods follow:

   • base your scores on the students' success in correcting MUG Shot paragraphs;

   • ask students to file their corrected sentences and paragraphs in their journals so you can give the work summative grades, basing your scores on how thoroughly corrections are made;

   • ask students to file corrected sentences and paragraphs in their journals so you can evaluate the work, basing your scores on the students' abilities to correct these errors in their own writing.

Additional Activities

6. For additional MUG Shot sentences and paragraphs, contact the Great Source Education Group at 1-800-289-4490, and ask for Write Source's *Level 12 Daily Language Workouts*. This book contains all the MUG Shot sentences and paragraphs included in this section of the Instructor's Manual, plus additional sentences and paragraphs. (The *Level 12 Daily Language Workouts* also contains writing prompts, sentence modeling activities, and guidelines for keeping journals and learning logs.)

MUG SHOT SENTENCES: PUNCTUATION

- **Commas (Appositive and Independent Clauses), Spelling**

  Typewriters, originaly designed as writing machines for the blind became popular in the business world in the 1880s, and created many new jobs for women.

- **Hyphen (Fraction), Comma (Appositive), Spelling, Usage (Right Word)**

  Alaska, the largest state with the fewest people has one third of it's land inside the Artic Circle.

- **Commas (Restrictive Phrase and Adverb Clause), Hyphen (Life Span)**

  Humorist, Mark Twain (1835,1910) wore white linen suits in summer and in winter, because they made him feel "clean in a dirty world."

- **Colon (Quotation), Direct Quotation, Commas (Independent Clauses and Appositive), Spelling**

  Harriet Tubman, the former slave who became famous for her corage as a conductor on the Underground Railroad once made this statement "On my Underground Railroad I never ran my train off the track and I never lost a passenger".

- **Hyphen (Single-Thought Adjective), Spelling, Colon (To Introduce Explanatory List), Apostrophe (Possession)**

  According to a well publicized goverment report, more than half of Americas' new jobs will be in the following industries, health services, business services, and retail trade.

CORRECTED SENTENCES

- **Commas (Appositive and Independent Clauses), Spelling**

  Typewriters, originally designed as writing machines for the blind, became popular in the business world in the 1880s and created many new jobs for women.

- **Hyphen (Fraction), Comma (Appositive), Spelling, Usage (Right Word)**

  Alaska, the largest state with the fewest people, has one-third of its land inside the Arctic Circle.

- **Commas (Restrictive Phrase and Adverb Clause), Hyphen (Life Span)**

  Humorist Mark Twain (1835-1910) wore white linen suits in summer and in winter because they made him feel "clean in a dirty world."

- **Colon (Quotation), Direct Quotation, Commas (Independent Clauses and Appositive), Spelling**

  Harriet Tubman, the former slave who became famous for her courage as a conductor on the Underground Railroad, once made this statement: "On my Underground Railroad I never ran my train off the track, and I never lost a passenger."

- **Hyphen (Single-Thought Adjective), Spelling, Colon (To Introduce Explanatory List), Apostrophe (Possession)**

  According to a well-publicized government report, more than half of America's new jobs will be in the following industries: health services, business services, and retail trade.

Twain and Technology

Mark Twain, Americas best loved humourist once said that he felt like "the most conspicuous person on the planet". He was a man who loved technology, but often lacked good business sense. Given a chance to invest in Alexander Graham Bells new invention, the telephone he decided it was too risky. Later, he became the first person to have a telephone in a private home, and delighted in using his new contraption day and night. Though Twain went bankcrupt several times through his ill fated investments in gagets, he became a rich man and a world famos celebrity through his writing and lecturing. His 19 room mansion in Hartford, Connecticut, had many oddities, including a black bed carved with angels that was big enough for the hole family to sleep in.

Twain and Technology

Mark Twain, America's best loved humourist **humorist,** once said that he felt like "the most conspicuous person on the planet". He was a man who loved technology, but often lacked good business sense. Given a chance to invest in Alexander Graham Bell's new invention, the telephone, he decided it was too risky. Later, he became the first person to have a telephone in a private home, and delighted in using his new contraption day and night. Though Twain went **bankrupt** several times through his ill fated investments in **gadgets** gagets, he became a rich man and a world **famous** celebrity through his writing and lecturing. His 19 room mansion in Hartford, Connecticut, had many oddities, including a black bed carved with angels that was big enough for the **whole** hole family to sleep in.

MUG SHOT SENTENCES: CAPITALIZATION AND FRAGMENTS

- **Capitalization, Fragment, Comma (Introductory Adverb Clause)**

If ice did not float. (this is called a hypothetical question) Tons of it at both the north pole and the south pole would sink, covering the earth with water.

- **Capitalization, Fragment, Hyphens (Single-Thought Adjective)**

The Houston rockets won back to back championships. In the nba (National Basketball Association) in 1994 and 1995.

- **Capitalization, Commas (Restrictive Phrase and Introductory Phrase), Spelling, Quotation Marks (Single), Punctuation (Magazine Title)**

In an article for the british magazine, The Idler Helen Wilkinson writes, "Many young people critisize their managers for their "make-work" rather than "real-work" mentality."

- **Capitalization, Fragment, End Punctuation, Comma (Address), Spelling**

"R U confused" is the acual name of a Booklet written by a Senior English class at Fair haven Union high school in Fair haven, Vermont. Explaining the mysteries of the S.a.t. exam.

- **Capitalization, Fragment, Comma (Appositive), Parentheses, Spelling**

John Adams and Thomas Jefferson, our second and third Presidents both died on the fourth of July in 1826. On the 50th Anniversery of the signing of the Decleration of Independance (isn't that amazing?).

CORRECTED SENTENCES

● **Capitalization, Fragment, Comma (Introductory Adverb Clause)**

If ice did not float (this is called a hypothetical question), tons of it at both the North Pole and the South Pole would sink, covering the earth with water.

● **Capitalization, Fragment, Hyphens (Single-Thought Adjective)**

The Houston Rockets won back-to-back championships in the NBA (National Basketball Association) in 1994 and 1995.

● **Capitalization, Commas (Restrictive Phrase and Introductory Phrase), Spelling, Quotation Marks (Single), Punctuation (Magazine Title)**

In an article for the British magazine The Idler, Helen Wilkinson writes, "Many young people criticize their managers for their 'make-work' rather than 'real-work' mentality."

● **Capitalization, Fragment, End Punctuation, Comma (Address), Spelling**

"R U Confused?" is the actual name of a booklet written by a senior English class at Fair Haven Union High School in Fair Haven, Vermont, explaining the mysteries of the SAT exam.

(SAT could also be written S.A.T.)

● **Capitalization, Fragment, Comma (Appositive), Parentheses, Spelling**

John Adams and Thomas Jefferson, our second and third presidents, both died on the Fourth of July in 1826 on the 50th anniversary of the signing of the Declaration of Independence. (Isn't that amazing?)

MUG SHOT PARAGRAPHS

Wanted: Time Out

Job seekers under 30 dont want to become workaholics enslaved to a workplace, that provides zero security from layoffs at any moment. That's what Helen Wilkinson, a british writer featured in the magazine utne reader believes. Citing a book called The intimate History of Humanity. Wilkinson says that young people want something their parents never had—control of their time. Can anyone blame them for not wanting to make winning a gold watch from general motors or ibm the Supreme Goal of their lives? Whether they're from the north, south, east, or west, they're looking for new ways to live and work. Says Wilkinson (And I agree), "we must ask what needs to be done to speed up the process of breaking free from the tyranny of to little time".

CORRECTED PARAGRAPH

Wanted: Time Out

Job seekers under 30 don't want to become workaholics enslaved to a workplace that provides zero security from layoffs at any moment. That's what Helen Wilkinson, a British writer featured in the magazine Utne Reader, believes. Citing a book called The Intimate History of Humanity, Wilkinson says that young people want something their parents never had—control of their time. Can anyone blame them for not wanting to make winning a gold watch from General Motors or IBM the Supreme Goal of their lives? Whether they're from the North, South, East, or West, they're looking for new ways to live and work. Says Wilkinson (And I agree), "We must ask what needs to be done to speed up the process of breaking free from the tyranny of too little time".

MUG SHOT SENTENCES: CAPITALIZATION AND COMMA SPLICES

● **Capitalization, Comma Splice, Commas (Address and Conjunctive Adverb)**

On his deathbed, the philosopher socrates said, "I am not an athenian [a resident of Athens Greece] nor a Greek but a Citizen of the World," nevertheless he was executed for supposedly corrupting the minds of young Athenians.

● **Capitalization, Comma Splice, Commas (Series and Conjunctive Adverb), Spelling**

Many seniors have dicided not to go on the class trip to Arizona, nicknamed the Apache State for the number of native americans who live there, consequently these Classmates won't see the painted dessert, the petrified forest or the grand canyon.

● **Capitalization, Comma Splice, Hyphen (Single-Thought Adjective), Spelling**

In her mid-30's, aunt Yolanda made a u-turn and, without the benefit of even one busyness course, went from full time Mother and President of the pta to ceo of her own small company, we're very proud of her.

● **Capitalization, Comma Splice, Spelling, Usage (Right Word)**

Islam, a major world religion, is dominent in the middle east, it's followers are called muslims, and it's sacred book is the koran.

● **Capitalization, Comma Splice, Commas (Address and Appositive), Spelling**

My Grandfather a world War II veteran heard president Truman anounce that the United States had dropped the first atomic bomb on hiroshima Japan, three days later, a second a-bomb was dropped on nagasaki.

CORRECTED SENTENCES

- **Capitalization, Comma Splice, Commas (Address and Conjunctive Adverb)**

On his deathbed, the philosopher Socrates said, "I am not an Athenian [a resident of Athens, Greece] nor a Greek but a citizen of the world." Nevertheless, he was executed for supposedly corrupting the minds of young Athenians.

(The comma splice could also be corrected with a semicolon placed outside the quotation marks.)

- **Capitalization, Comma Splice, Commas (Series and Conjunctive Adverb), Spelling**

Many seniors have decided not to go on the class trip to Arizona, nicknamed the Apache State for the number of Native Americans who live there; consequently, these classmates won't see the Painted Desert, the Petrified Forest, or the Grand Canyon.

(The comma splice could also be corrected by creating two sentences.)

- **Capitalization, Comma Splice, Hyphen (Single-Thought Adjective), Spelling**

In her mid-30's, Aunt Yolanda made a U-turn and, without the benefit of even one business course, went from full-time mother and president of the PTA to CEO of her own small company. We're very proud of her.

(The comma splice could also be corrected with a semicolon.)

- **Capitalization, Comma Splice, Spelling, Usage (Right Word)**

Islam, a major world religion, is dominant in the Middle East; its followers are called Muslims, and its sacred book is the Koran.

(The comma splice could also be corrected by creating two sentences.)

- **Capitalization, Comma Splice, Commas (Address and Appositive), Spelling**

My grandfather, a World War II veteran, heard President Truman announce that the United States had dropped the first atomic bomb on Hiroshima, Japan. Three days later, a second A-bomb was dropped on Nagasaki.

(The comma splice could also be corrected with a semicolon.)

Small-Business Success

Do you need an mba (masters in Business administration) to start up a small business and be successful? My uncle Jim says "I wasn't the type of guy who gets promoted at ibm or nordstrom's. I learned about business by working in my parents' chinese restaurant, I learned about business by reading the Wall street Journal". At his mom and dad's resterant, the Dragon Inn south, he learned everything from working the cash register to making eggrolls, since those early days he moved to Florida where he and his wife started a successful travel agency, catering to asian American tourists. My Uncle says "Tourists enjoy everything from St. Augustine in the Northeastern part of the state to the Everglades national park in the Southwestern part." Walt Disney world, however, is the favorit place. "No other place even comes close", Jim says.

Small-Business Success

Do you need an ~~mba~~ MBA (masters in Business administration) to start up a small business and be successful? My uncle Jim says, "I wasn't the type of guy who gets promoted at ~~ibm~~ IBM or Nordstrom's. I learned about business by working in my parents' Chinese restaurant. I learned about business by reading the Wall Street Journal." At his mom and dad's ~~resterant~~ restaurant, the Dragon Inn South, he learned everything from working the cash register to making eggrolls. Since those early days, he moved to Florida where he and his wife started a successful travel agency, catering to Asian American tourists. My Uncle says, "Tourists enjoy everything from St. Augustine in the Northeastern part of the state to the Everglades National Park in the Southwestern part." Walt Disney World, however, is the ~~favorit~~ favorite place. "No other place even comes close," Jim says.

MUG SHOT SENTENCES: RAMBLING AND RUN-ON SENTENCES

● **Rambling Sentence, Commas (Explanatory Phrase and Independent Clauses), Spelling**

The shop-till-you-drop urge can sometimes become an obsession, and a support group Debtors Anonamous similar to Alcoholics Anonamous, exists and people who have maxed out their credit cards, and morgaged their lives discover that they have plenty of company.

● **Rambling Sentence, Comma (Coordinate Adjectives), Spelling**

The Internet and cyberspace are now as clogged with traffic as most city highways at rush hour and users often experiance major delays in getting information and people's high expectations are often disapointed by the lack of speedy dependable service.

● **Run-on Sentence, Commas (Series), Spelling**

Ethnocentrism is an additude that makes people believe that their race, culture class or nation is superior to all others when this additude is carried to extremes, persecutions or even war can resilt.

● **Rambling Sentence, Spelling, Usage (Right Word), Comma (Introductory Adverb Clause)**

When you're car overheats and steam billows out from under the hood you need to remember that payshunce is a virtue and don't immediately remove the radiator cap, or you may get scalded.

● **Run-on Sentence, Capitalization, Spelling**

Vegetarians can enjoy Summer barbecues without feeling left out grilling is not just for meat anymore skewered marinated vegatables are delishous when grilled.

CORRECTED SENTENCES

(Answers will vary for correcting rambling and run-on sentences.)

- **Rambling Sentence, Commas (Explanatory Phrase and Independent Clauses), Spelling**

  The shop-till-you-drop urge can sometimes become an obsession. A support group, Debtors Anonymous, similar to Alcoholics Anonymous, exists. People who have maxed out their credit cards and mortgaged their lives discover that they have plenty of company.

- **Rambling Sentence, Comma (Coordinate Adjectives), Spelling**

  The Internet and cyberspace are now as clogged with traffic as most city highways at rush hour. Users often experience major delays in getting information. People's high expectations are often disappointed by the lack of speedy, dependable service.

- **Run-on Sentence, Commas (Series), Spelling**

  Ethnocentrism is an attitude that makes people believe that their race, culture, class, or nation is superior to all others. When this attitude is carried to extremes, persecutions or even war can result.

- **Rambling Sentence, Spelling, Usage (Right Word), Comma (Introductory Adverb Clause)**

  When your car overheats and steam billows out from under the hood, you need to remember that patience is a virtue. Don't immediately remove the radiator cap, or you may get scalded.

- **Run-on Sentence, Capitalization, Spelling**

  Vegetarians can enjoy summer barbecues without feeling left out. Grilling is not just for meat anymore. Skewered marinated vegetables are delicious when grilled.

The Rush to Get On-Line

In the early 1980s federal express was the messenger of choise and in the late 1980s, fax machines took over that title and in the last years of the twentieth censury however the Internet is suppose to become a kind of global super-messenger. The Internet a worldwide network of interconnected computers is growing at a faster pace than any form of telecommunications ever has, including the telephone it is estimated that by 1998 the user base will be 100,000,000. On the Internet you can send and recieve personal mail, acess all kinds of information and post messages for all to see and even though learning too effectively use the Internet is definitly harder than running a vcr, everybody, it seems, wants to get in on the action.

The Rush to Get On-Line

In the early 1980s ~~f~~ederal ~~e~~xpress was the messenger of ~~choise~~ *choice* and in the late 1980s fax machines took over that title and ~~in~~ the last years of the twentieth ~~censury~~ *century* however, the Internet is ~~suppose~~ *supposed* to become a kind of global super-messenger. The Internet, a worldwide network of interconnected computers is growing at a faster pace than any form of telecommunications ever has, including the telephone, ~~it~~ is estimated that by 1998 the user base will be ~~100,000,000~~ *100 million*. On the Internet you can send and recieve personal mail, ~~acess~~ *access* all kinds of information and post messages for all to see, ~~and~~ ~~e~~ven though learning ~~too~~ *to* effectively use the Internet is ~~definitly~~ *definitely* harder than running a ~~ver~~ *VCR*, everybody, it seems, wants to get in on the action.

MUG SHOT SENTENCES: PRONOUN PROBLEMS

● **Pronoun/Antecedent Agreement, Usage (Right Word), Spelling**

Everyone needs to improve their writeing and math skills because less and less jobs require mussels only

● **Pronoun (Nominative Case), Pronoun/Antecedent Agreement, Usage (Right Word), Comma Splice**

Her and I discovered that before the Revolutionary War, anyone who needed money had to borrow from there friends and family, no banks existed.

● **Pronoun/Antecedent Agreement, Comma (Series), Spelling**

American shopping malls are amazing places where people can shop register to vote, give blood, play video games attend a worship service of your choice, get married or mail a letter.

● **Pronoun/Antecedent Agreement, Spelling, Capitalization**

If a worker is unable to work because of a savere disability, social security offers monthly disability payments until they are able to work again.

● **Pronoun (Objective Case), Spelling, Substandard Language**

Either ratios or percentages may be use to express the liklihood that an accident will happen to you or I when driving.

CORRECTED SENTENCES

- **Pronoun/Antecedent Agreement, Usage (Right Word), Spelling**

Everyone needs to improve his or her writing and math skills because fewer and fewer jobs require muscles only.

(OR: All workers [students, people, etc.] need to improve their . . .)

- **Pronoun (Nominative Case), Pronoun/Antecedent Agreement, Usage (Right Word), Comma Splice**

She and I discovered that before the Revolutionary War, people who needed money had to borrow from their friends and family; no banks existed.

(The comma splice could also be corrected by creating two sentences. The antecedent agreement error could also be corrected by keeping the singular "anyone" and changing "their friends and family" to "her or his friends and family.")

- **Pronoun/Antecedent Agreement, Comma (Series), Spelling**

American shopping malls are amazing places where people can shop, register to vote, give blood, play video games, attend a worship service of their choice, get married, or mail a letter.

- **Pronoun/Antecedent Agreement, Spelling, Capitalization**

If a worker is unable to work because of a severe disability, Social Security offers monthly disability payments until he or she is able to work again.

- **Pronoun (Objective Case), Spelling, Substandard Language**

Either ratios or percentages may be used to express the likelihood that an accident will happen to you or me when driving.

Social Insecurity

Social Security which I figured had been around just about forever came along in the 1930s when millions of people were out of work. Social Security was one of President Roosevelts New Deal programs aimed at putting the American economy back on their feet, Social Security ain't welfare. A worker and their employer pay taxes based on salary. In most situations, people end up being part of the system whether he or she wants to be part of it or not. Just about everyone accept the very rich rely on Social Security. My grandparents and me think Social Security is a great deal for them, but my sister and me worry that it will be no deal when people my age reach his or her golden years.

CORRECTED PARAGRAPH

Social Insecurity

Social Security‸which I figured had been around just about forever‸

came along in the 1930s when millions of people were out of work. Social

Security was one of President Roosevelt's New Deal programs aimed at

putting the American economy back on ~~their~~ *its* feet. Social Security ~~ain't~~ *isn't*

welfare. ~~A worker~~ *Workers* and their ~~employer~~ *employers* pay taxes based on salary. In most

situations, people end up being part of the system whether ~~he or she~~ *they*

wants to be part of it or not. Just about everyone ~~accept~~ *except* the very rich

~~rely~~ *relies* on Social Security. My grandparents and ~~me~~ *I* think Social Security is

a great deal for them, but my sister and ~~me~~ *I* worry that it will be no deal

when people my age reach ~~his or her~~ *their* golden years.

(Remember: Agreement problems can usually be corrected in more than one
way.)

MUG SHOT SENTENCES: VERB PROBLEMS

● **Subject/Verb Agreement, Spelling, Comma Splice, Usage (Right Word)**

Breatheing and swallowing is impossable to do simultanyously, set down and try it some time.

● **Verb Tense, Capitalization, Spelling, Hyphen, Apostrophe (Possession)**

Niether soviet leader Mikhail Gorbachev nor the countrys most powerful generals are able to prevent the collapse of the Soviet Union during the 1989,1990 time span.

● **Subject/Verb Agreement, Punctuation (Title of a Painting), Spelling, Number (Beginning a Sentence)**

3 layers of paint lies under the surface of the Mona Lisa, the famus painting by Leonardo da Vinci.

● **Verb Tense, Subject/Verb Agreement, Usage (Right Word), Rambling Sentence**

Everybody fighting the battle of the bulge know that celery is on the side of thin people everywhere and that chewing a stalk of celery took more energy then the celery itself contains and so pass the salt!

● **Subject/Verb Agreement, Usage (Right Word), Quotation Marks, Apostrophe (Possession)**

In business its good to remember the following words attributed to Dale Carnegie: "A persons name are to them the sweetest and most important sound in any language.

CORRECTED SENTENCES

- **Subject/Verb Agreement, Spelling, Comma Splice, Usage (Right Word)**

  Breathing and swallowing are impossible to do simultaneously. Sit down and try it some time.

  (The comma splice could also be corrected with a semicolon.)

- **Verb Tense, Capitalization, Spelling, Hyphen, Apostrophe (Possession)**

  Neither Soviet leader Mikhail Gorbachev nor the country's most powerful generals were able to prevent the collapse of the Soviet Union during the 1989-1990 time span.

- **Subject/Verb Agreement, Punctuation (Title of a Painting), Spelling, Number (Beginning a Sentence)**

  Three layers of paint lie under the surface of the <u>Mona Lisa</u>, the famous painting by Leonardo da Vinci.

- **Verb Tense, Subject/Verb Agreement, Usage (Right Word), Rambling Sentence**

  Everybody fighting the battle of the bulge knows that celery is on the side of thin people everywhere. Chewing a stalk of celery takes more energy than the celery itself contains. So pass the salt!

- **Subject/Verb Agreement, Usage (Right Word), Quotation Marks, Apostrophe (Possession)**

  In business it's good to remember the following words attributed to Dale Carnegie: "A person's name is to that person the sweetest and most important sound in any language."

Slow Start for <u>Mona Lisa</u>

One of the most famous paintings of all time are the Mona Lisa. Perfect poise and misterious beauty is two phrases use to describe the woman in the painting. She has however no eyebrows, it was the fashion in Florence during the renaissance to shave eyebrows off. The painting, which is so large in our minds and imaginations, are in reality less than 2 feet by 2 feet. Leonardo da Vinci takes so long (four years) to complete the painting that the Florentine merchant whom commissioned the portrait of his third wife, Lisa, gets impatient. He refuses to pay for the painting, which is today priceless. Leonardo according to tradition sold the painting to the king of France. Is the woman in the painting smiling or does she have some other secret we will never know. Seated in her misty, mountainous landscape, she remains aloof and misterious forever.

Slow Start for <u>Mona Lisa</u>

One of the most famous paintings of all time ~~are~~ *is* the <u>Mona Lisa</u>. Perfect poise and ~~misterious~~ *mysterious* beauty ~~is~~ *are* two phrases ~~use~~ *used* to describe the woman in the painting. She has, however, no eyebrows; it was the fashion in Florence during the *R*enaissance to shave eyebrows off. The painting, which is so large in our minds and imaginations, ~~are~~ *is* in reality less than ~~2~~ *two* feet by ~~2~~ *two* feet. Leonardo da Vinci ~~takes~~ *took* so long (four years) to complete the painting that the Florentine merchant ~~whom~~ *who* commissioned the portrait of his third wife, Lisa, ~~gets~~ *got* impatient. He ~~refuses~~ *refused* to pay for the painting, which is today priceless. Leonardo, according to tradition, sold the painting to the king of France. Is the woman in the painting smiling, or does she have some other secret we will never know? Seated in her misty, mountainous landscape, she remains aloof and ~~misterious~~ *mysterious* forever.

MUG SHOT SENTENCES: CLICHES, SEXISM, AND PARALLEL STRUCTURE

- **Cliches, Comma (Introductory Adverb Clause)**

  Because she was hungry as a bear she blew her stack quick as a flash.

- **Sexism, Colon (To Introduce Explanatory List), Comma (Series), Spelling, Usage (Right Word)**

  Its vary common to exempt the following classes of people from jury duty pharmacists phisicians clergymen policemen firemen and attorneys.

- **Parallel Structure, Usage (Right Word), Commas (Numbers and Series), Hyphen (Fraction)**

  Full-grown mail polar bears way up to 1500 pounds live to be up to 25 years old and up to four and one half inches is how thick their blubber can be.

- **Sexism, Deadwood, Comma (Introductory Adverb Clause), Spelling, Hyphen (Single-Thought Adjective)**

  If man neglects his fundamental, basic principals when making future plans the end result can range from an uneasy feeling to a full blown sudden crisus or terrible tragidy.

- **Parallel Structure, Comma (Coordinate Adjectives), Pronoun/Antecedent Agreement, Colon (To Introduce Explanatory Sentence)**

  The orb weaver spider weaves beautiful well-engineered webs, first, they make a frame, filling the in frame with a hub and spokes comes next, and finally they coat the entire web with a sticky adhesive.

CORRECTED SENTENCES

- **Cliches, Comma (Introductory Adverb Clause)**

  Because she was very hungry, she quickly lost her temper.

- **Sexism, Colon (To Introduce Explanatory List), Comma (Series), Spelling, Usage (Right Word)**

  It's very common to exempt the following classes of people from jury duty: pharmacists, physicians, clergy, police, fire fighters, and attorneys.

- **Parallel Structure, Usage (Right Word), Commas (Numbers and Series), Hyphen (Fraction)**

  Full-grown male polar bears weigh up to 1,500 pounds, live to be up to 25 years old, and have blubber up to four and one-half inches thick.

- **Sexism, Deadwood, Comma (Introductory Adverb Clause), Spelling, Hyphen (Single-Thought Adjective)**

  If we neglect our principles when making plans, the result can range from an uneasy feeling to a full-blown crisis or tragedy.

  (OR: If people . . . their principles . . .; If a person . . . his or her principles)

- **Parallel Structure, Comma (Coordinate Adjectives), Pronoun/Antecedent Agreement, Colon (To Introduce Explanatory Sentence)**

  The orb weaver spider weaves beautiful, well-engineered webs: first, it makes a frame, next it fills in the frame with a hub and spokes, and finally it coats the entire web with a sticky adhesive.

  (OR: Orb weaver spiders weave . . . they make . . .)

Bear Facts

Unlike man, bears they take a long Winter rest. They do not truly hibernate however, they're temperature remains almost normal and they forage for food on warm days. A pregnant female bear is in fact busy as a bee during the period of time she gives birth to her cubs in January or Febuary. Her first birth is usually a single cub, in subsequent births she will have two, three, or having four cubs at once is even possible. Each of the baby bears are tiny in size weighing less then a pound. It has no hair no eyesight and teeth arent even present. All it does for a hole month is eat and sleep. A cub will stay with it's mother until after the following years Winter rest.

Bear Facts

Unlike ~~man~~ humans, bears ~~they~~ take a long Winter rest. They do not truly

hibernate, however, ~~they're~~ Their temperature remains almost normal, and they

forage for food on warm days. A pregnant female bear is in fact, ~~busy as~~ , very busy

~~a bee~~ during the ~~period of~~ time she gives birth to her cubs in January or

~~Febuary~~ February. Her first birth is usually a single cub, in subsequent births she

will have two, three, or ~~having~~ even four cubs at once, ~~is even possible~~. Each

of the baby bears ~~are~~ is tiny, ~~in size~~ weighing less ~~then~~ than a pound. It has no

hair, no eyesight, and ~~teeth~~ no ~~arent even present~~. All it does for a ~~hole~~ whole

month is eat and sleep. A cub will stay with ~~it's~~ its mother until after the

following year's Winter rest.

Additional Sources

These sources offer helpful information on the following topics.

Assessment

Black, Laurel, Donald Daiker, Jeffrey Sommers, and Gail Stygall, eds. *New Directions in Portfolio Assessment: Reflective Practice, Critical Theory and Large Scale Scoring.* Portsmouth, NH: Boynton/Cook, 1994.

Elbow, Peter. "Ranking, Evaluating, and Linking: Sorting Out Three Forms of Judgment." *College English* 55 (1993): 187-206.

White, Edward. *Teaching and Assessing Writing.* 2nd ed. San Francisco: Jossey-Bass, 1994.

Wiggins, Grant. *Assessing Student Performance: Exploring the Purpose and Limits of Testing.* San Francisco: Jossey-Bass, 1993.

Yancey, Kathleen Blake, ed. *Portfolios in the Writing Classroom: An Introduction.* Urbana, IL: NCTE, 1992.

Creative Writing

Eco, Umberto. *Six Walks in the Fictional Woods.* Cambridge, MA: Harvard, 1994.

Lynn, Steven. *Texts and Contexts: Writing About Literature with Critical Theory.* New York: HarperCollins, 1994.

Wallace, Robert. *Writing Poems.* 3rd ed. New York: HarperCollins, 1991.

Welty, Eudora. *One Writer's Beginnings.* Cambridge, MA: Harvard, 1984.

Grammar and Style

Flood, James, et al., eds. *Handbook of Research on Teaching the English Language Arts.* New York: Macmillan, 1991.

Hickey, Dona J. *Developing a Written Voice.* Palo Alto, CA: Mayfield, 1993.

Hillocks, Jr. George. *Research on Written Composition.* Urbana, IL: ERIC, 1986.

Noguchi, Rei R. *Grammar and the Teaching of Writing: Limits and Possibilities.* Urbana, IL: NCTE, 1991.

Williams, Joseph M. *Style: Ten Lessons in Clarity and Grace.* New York: HarperCollins, 1994.

Pedagogical Strategies

Duffy, Donna Killian, and Janet Wright Jones. *Teaching Within the Rhythms of the Semester.* San Francisco: Jossey-Bass, 1995.

Goodsell, Anne S., et al. *Collaborative Learning: A Sourcebook for Higher Education.* Vol 1. University Park, PA: National Center for Postsecondary Teaching, Learning, and Assessment, 1992.

Jones, Elizabeth A. *Goals Inventories: Writing, Speech Communication, and Critical Thinking.* University Park, PA: National Center for Postsecondary Teaching, Learning, and Assessment, 1994.

Kadel, Stephanie, and Julia A. Keechner. *Collaborative Learning: A Sourcebook for Higher Education.* Vol, 2. University Park, PA: National Center for Postsecondary Teaching, Learning, and Assessment, 1994.

Meyers, Chet, and Thomas B. Jones. *Promoting Active Learning: Strategies for the College Classroom.* San Francisco: Jossey-Bass, 1993.

Writing Across the Curriculum

Fulwiler, Toby, and Art Young, eds. *Programs That Work.* Portsmouth, NH: Heinemann/Boynton/Cook, 1990.

Howard, Rebecca, and Sandra Jamieson. *The Bedford Guide to Teaching Writing in the Disciplines.* Boston, MA: Bedford Books, 1995.

McLeod, Susan, ed. *Strengthening Programs in Writing Across the Curriculum.* San Francisco: Jossey-Bass, 1988.

Thaiss, Christopher. *The Harcourt Brace Guide to Writing Across the Curriculum.* New York: Harcourt Brace, 1997.

Walvoord, Barbara, et al. eds. *In the Long Run: A Study of Faculty in Three WAC Programs.* Urbana, IL: NCTE, 1997.

Index